The Complete Lakeland Walker

Tom Bowker

Dalesman

First Published in Great Britain 1993 by
Dalesman Publishing Company Limited,
Stable Courtyard, Broughton Hall,
Skipton, North Yorkshire BD23 3AE
Text and drawings © 1993 **Tom Bowker**

ISBN **1 85568 053 X**
Typeset by **Lands Services, East Molesey, Surrey.**
Printed by **Lavenham Press, Lavenham, Suffolk.**

CONTENTS

KEY TO MAPS

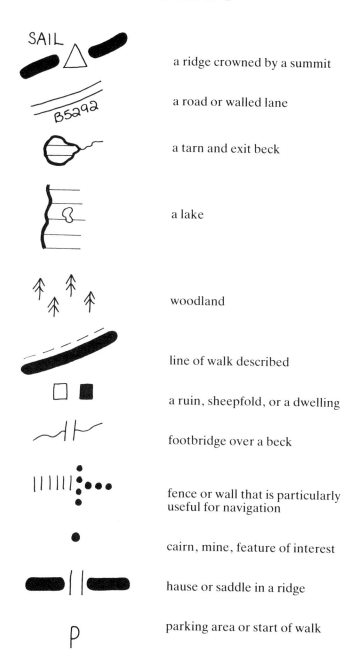

a ridge crowned by a summit

a road or walled lane

a tarn and exit beck

a lake

woodland

line of walk described

a ruin, sheepfold, or a dwelling

footbridge over a beck

fence or wall that is particularly useful for navigation

cairn, mine, feature of interest

hause or saddle in a ridge

parking area or start of walk

INTRODUCTION

THIS book is a selection of favourite Lakeland walks taken from the popular series of Dalesman's 'Walks From Your Car' books.

It is not aimed at the motorist who is looking for a short stroll in their driving shoes, nor is it aimed at the hardened long-distance fellwalker. Rather, it is aimed at the fellwalking beginner, the motorist-cum-walker who is prepared to sling a pack on their back and pull on a pair of boots for a few hours' exercise, or for families who are introducing their children to the fells.

The "bagging" of summits is just one facet of the walks described. There are tarns and pools for bathing, woods, waterfalls, old quarries and workshops to explore, lovely impromptu picnic spots, all of which should appeal to children of all ages.

All of the walks are circular, starting and finishing at the same point but returning by a different route in order to add interest. The walks are roughly divided into three types:-

1) **VALLEY WALKS.** The very nature of Lakeland makes genuine valley walks hard to find, for sooner or later you have to start climbing. Selected under this heading are 'true' valley walks plus a handful that bend the rules slightly. For these walks, light footgear could be worn in dry conditions, but boots or stout walking shoes are advised.

2) **MEDIUM WALKS.** These are walks which climb one or more summits over one thousand but below two thousand feet above sea level. They form the bulk of the walks in the book for I felt they would appeal most to the kind of walkers described above. They do, however, cover similar terrain to the 'Fell Walks' and strictly speaking the same rules about clothing and footgear described below apply here.

3) **FELL WALKS.** These are walks which climb one or more summits over two thousand, or three thousand, feet above sea level. They are not, however, strenuous walks of their type, either being of no great length or, with exceptions, over relatively easy ground, and easier options or 'escape' routes are described. Nevertheless, they should all be treated with respect, especially in bad weather or winter conditions. Boots should be worn and rucksacks contain waterproof/windproof cagoule and overtrousers, food and drink, spare clothing, map, compass, whistle, simple first aid kit, and survival bag.

In winter a torch, balaclava, mittens and some extra food should be added. All these walks could be potentially dangerous under icy or hard snow conditions and, given such conditions apply, it is strongly advised that Walks 18, 19, 25 and 27 in particular are left well alone unless you possess ice-axe and crampons and the skill to use them. It is advised that you learn the use of map and compass, particularly if you plan walking the high fells in winter. Remember the golden rule – start using your compass from a point where you know where you are, don't wait until you are lost. Never be afraid to turn back if the weather deteriorates.

Each walk is illustrated by a rough sketch-map to be used in conjunction with the text. It is advisable, however, also to carry the relevant sheet of the 1:25000, 2½"-1 mile, The English Lakes Outdoor Leisure maps. All the place names in the text refer to an edition of these maps. The mileages are approximate and 'left' or 'right' refers to a physical feature as if facing it. All the walks described are on official rights-of-way, permissive footpaths or public access areas. Paths can, however, be legally changed from time to time, in which case there should be a signpost specifically indicating any alteration. Limited space means I have to choose between detailed route descriptions, incidental information, and detailed descriptions of views. I tend to be niggardly with the latter, feeling it's useful for fellwalkers to orientate the view to the map.

I make every effort to keep walk descriptions up to date, but the more books I write the more monumental the task, especially on the lower walks where 'forestry', for example, may alter the siting of paths, stiles, etc. Should you find any appreciable difference to the description and would inform me via the publisher, you will receive my grateful thanks.

Nine years ago I was given the opportunity to start a series of 'Walks From Your Car' books. For decades prior to that my interest had largely been confined to the high fells. If the fell was below two thousand feet I didn't really want to know. Over the past nine years I have discovered corners of Lakeland that have delighted me and I hope will delight you. My love for mountain country extends beyond Lakeland but here it was nurtured, and this crumpled corner of England is as much a part of me as my right arm. Just get out there and let the fells soak into your soul. Remember – "But mind chains do not clank where one's next neighbour is the sky." Happy walking.

Tom Bowker

CONISTON

Walk 1

Fell Walk, 6-7 miles

Coniston Old Man and Dow Crag

This is a fine walk which reaches the summit of one of Lakeland's most popular peaks by a route which is slightly longer, but more interesting, than the 'tourist' route. It also crosses the summit of one of the major rock-climbing crags of Lakeland, giving the fellwalker a bird's-eye view of climbers in action. Unfortunately the early part of the walk is among the unsightly debris of industry, both ancient and modern. For those interested, however, it is an important part of the story of Lakeland and one cannot help but have admiration for man's skill, courage, and ingenuity in wresting riches from the obdurate rock.

Parking: Coniston village car park.

LEAVE the village by the lane running to the right of the Black Bull Hotel. After crossing a cattle-grid the surface deteriorates and soon the wall on the left falls back, giving good views down onto the cascades of Church Beck. Soon a fine bridge crossing the beck will be met and a footpath sign indicating Coniston Old Man that way. Ignore this and continue straight ahead, into Coppermines Valley. It is a drab place, its green flanks scarred and hacked and its floor piled with spoil heaps and ruined workings. We can however lift our eyes up to a superb skyline, seeing from left to right, Coniston Old Man, Brim Fell, Swirl How, and Wetherlam.

Eventually the path begins to climb, past the Youth Hostel on your right, and then an underground pumping-station on your left. Ahead you will see the fine cascades of Levers Water Beck; when the path begins to swing up to the right leave it and walk left to the footbridge at the foot of the falls. Cross this and turn right to climb up the obvious path slanting across the old spoil heaps that have spilled down from the grim portal of Simon's Nick above. This path gives a lovely view of the falls if they are in spate and ends on the crest of the Levers Water Dam. The scars of industry are left behind now, the eye is soothed by graceful mountain shapes and the ear by the soft lap of water. The flat grassy top of the dam is a fine picnic or sun-bathing spot and the boulders of its facing make useful diving platforms.

The saddle at the head of the valley beyond the tarn is Swirl Hause, which divides the rugged mass of Wetherlam, on the right,

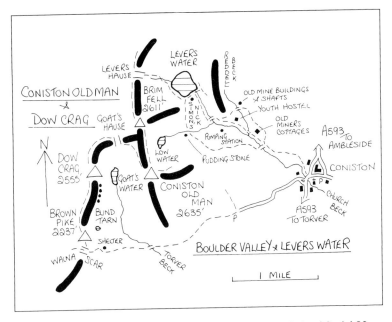

from more shapely Swirl How, on the left. To the left of Swirl How is the saddle of Levers Hause, your next objective. To the extreme left the summit and cairn of the Old Man may be glimpsed. Looking back there is a fine view down onto Coniston Water and beyond, across the wooded hills of South Lakeland, to the distant Pennines, with the hump of Ingleborough predominant.

To continue walk along the crest of the dam, passing the fenced-off chasm of Simon's Nick, reputedly a thousand feet deep. This is the most horrendous of the many shafts, tunnels, and quarries riddling these fells. They are interesting but they are dangerous, please be careful. Beyond the dam a path bears right, across boulders and scree, above the tarn and below the steep rocks of Gill Cove Crags. Follow this until Cove Beck is crossed when it turns steeply left and uphill. It is well cairned and eventually the angle eases as it climbs into Gill Cove but it steepens again for the final pull up to Levers Hause.

The tarn seen beyond the saddle is Seathwaite Tarn, above the Duddon Valley, beyond which rises the shapely peak of Harter Fell. Turn left here and follow the well-worn path along the broad ridge, bearing slightly east of south, to reach the summit cairn of Brim Fell. It is an easy walk now along to the summit of Coniston Old Man. There is a fine view down to your left into the blue depths of Low Water whilst over to your right the spiked summit of Dow Crag thrusts into view. A dip in the ridge reveals the great

10

crag with the blue dot of the Mountain Rescue Box at its foot giving some idea of scale. If a wish to return to Coniston is felt, from the summit of the Old Man, simply follow the eroded 'tourist' route leading down past Low Water and through the old quarries to meet the Walna Scar road and so back to Coniston Village.

For those who wish to continue, and the interest is certainly worth the extra expenditure of energy, retrace your steps for a short way until you see a path bearing away to your left. This slants down across steepening grassy slopes, above the dark waters of Goat's Water, to reach the broad grassy saddle of Goat's Hause. For those who wish it the walk can be shortened here by turning left down to the tarn, where a fine path along its eastern shore eventually leads on down to the Walna Scar track. To continue, however, follow the path swinging and climbing steeply left to reach the massive blocks that form the summit of Dow Crag. To the north-west the Scafells look particularly fine and to their left, on a clear day, the Isle of Man may be spotted.

Continue along the ridge, alongside an old wall at first, to reach the head of Great Gully. A circumspect peek over the edge gives some idea of the scale of the crag. Further down the ridge, from the rim of Easy Gully, a safer bird's-eye view may possibly be had of 'crag-rats' in action. The ridge climbs again to reach the summit of Brown Pike. Down to the left may be seen the tiny Blind Tarn, so-called because it has no outlet beck. From Brown Pike a worn stony path leads down to the crest of Walna Scar Pass. Turn left here and follow the worn track back to Coniston village. On your way you will get magnificent views of Dow Crag to your left, with the dark rift of Great Gully predominant.

Boulder Valley and Levers Water

*An amiable walk which passes through some remarkably rugged
mountain scenery to reach the shores of a lovely mountain tarn. For
those interested it also provides many aspects of the industrial history
of Lakeland, from the forbidding chasm of Simon's Nick to the
ruined mine-buildings of Red Dell and the Coppermines Valley.*

Parking: Coniston village car park.

FOLLOW the directions given in Walk 1 as far as the bridge over
Church Beck. You now cross this bridge and follow the path
slanting up the fellside to your right. You have a fine view of the
Coppermines Valley, with its spoil heaps, ruined mine-workings,
miners cottages (now holiday homes) and white-walled Youth
Hostel. Above it more mine buildings guard the entrance to Red
Dell, Wetherlam's high valley. Your path eventually joins a rough
road. Take the right fork. It is Alpine in character with steep crags
above to the left and the depths of Coppermines Valley below and
to the right. The road ends abruptly but a path continues on
heading towards a huge boulder perched on the edge of Low
Water Beck. You are now in Boulder Valley and the huge monolith apart (known as the Pudding Stone), it is easy to see why the
area got its name. The Pudding Stone can be climbed quite easily
from the rear. During filming of the TV game 'Treasure Hunt' its
star performer, Anneka Rice, was lowered onto its summit from a
helicopter. Curving around and above the valley are the rocky
ramparts of Coniston Old Man and Brim Fell, split in the middle
by the splendid cascades of Low Water Beck. These spill over the
lip of the corrie containing Low Water, above which the summit
ridge rears against the sky. To the right of the cascades the rugged
bastion of Raven Tor thrusts out from the summit of Brim Fell.

Cross the footbridge and follow the path up a grassy ridge to
reach the saddle at the foot of Raven Tor. From this saddle Levers
Water can be seen below. Hereabouts are several fenced-off mine
shafts and on a cold day warm air can be seen venting from the
bowels of the earth. Down to the right is Simon's Nick, reputedly a
thousand feet deep. Examine these shafts at a distance: **they are
extremely dangerous.** Go down to the dam and walk along it to the
far end. The view from the dam and its virtues as a picnic and
bathing spot are extolled in Walk 1. The easiest descent is to cross
the outlet from the tarn, if conditions allow, and turn right down
the Land Rover track on the far side of Levers Water Beck.

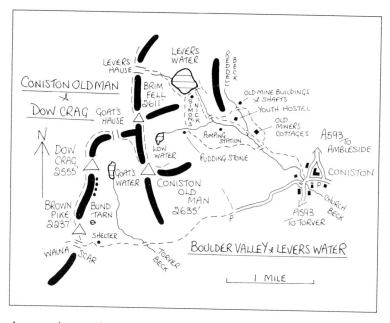

BOULDER VALLEY & LEVERS WATER

A more interesting way, however, is to leave the dam at a point where its rear wall meets the rocks and follow the path down the right-hand bank of the beck. This slants across the spoil heaps below the grim portal of Simon's Nick, with fine views of the waterfalls of the beck, to reach a footbridge at its foot. Cross the bridge to meet the Land Rover track. Turn right to follow the rough track back to Coppermines Valley and so back to Coniston. Soon after crossing the footbridge and following the track downhill a green miners' path will be seen branching off to your left. This provides an interesting alternative to the rough track. This path contours around Tongue Brow, before swinging left along the rim of a culvert cut by the miners, to cross Red Dell Beck just below the impressive mine-building guarding the entrance to Red Dell. Behind the ruin is a wide tunnel which can be entered as far as a barrier. Beyond the barrier is a deep shaft. Look for the winding gear above the shaft. The stone lined pit by the ruin probably once held a large water-wheel used for pumping water out of the shafts.

The path now contours along the left wall of Coppermines Valley, above and behind the old miners' cottages, before dropping down to rejoin the rough track just beyond the cottages.

Coniston Lakeshore, Torver and Walna Scar

This walk contrasts the sylvan beauty of the lakeshore with the rugged splendour of the high fells. Yet throughout it there is evidence of man's restless, ingenious energy, from sites of lake-shore bloomeries to the brooding chasms of Banishead Quarries.

Parking: Coniston village car park.

LEAVE the village by Lake Road leading to the steamer landing stage. Where the road bends left a footpath sign 'Coniston Hall', will be seen on the right. Cross the stile and, turning right, follow the hedgeline and yellow waymarkers to a gate in the corner of the field. Bear right through the gate. Beyond the hedge to the left will be seen the high chimneys of Coniston Hall. Soon the hedge falls back and you will come to a junction of paths in the middle of the field. Turn left and follow the path heading towards the hall. Pass in front and to the right of the building, towards a campsite. This Elizabethan manor-house was, in the 16th and 17th centuries, the home of the Lakeland family of Fleming but there was doubtless a dwelling-place on this site for many centuries before then.

As the path swings to the left a sign in a tree to the right indicates 'Public Footpath to Torver 2½ miles'. Follow the path through the campsite, bearing left, to reach the lake-shore. Across the lake the large white building is Brantwood, once the home of the artist and writer John Ruskin. Looking back towards Coniston from around this point there is a fine view of the fells with the rugged Yewdale Fells being particularly impressive. Beyond some boat-sheds the path eventually plunges into woods and for the next two miles or so twists and turns delightfully above the clear water of the lake. You will come across many tiny, shingly beaches, ideal for picnics and bathing. Care must be taken, however, for the shore shelves steeply to dangerous depths. Several 'bloomeries,' which were not sites where medieval nuns laundered their 'smalls' but rudimentary iron foundries, were sited hereabouts.

Eventually a wall is met, with a boathouse beyond it. Turn right here and follow a path running up alongside the wall to meet a fence. Turn right here to meet a gate which leads onto the A5084 Coniston-Greenodd road at the Torver Common car park. Turn right up the road, which climbs to pass a garage. Just beyond the garage, at a sharp corner, an overgrown bridleway leads down to your left. Follow this down to a bridge. As you descend a water-wheel will be seen in the beck to your right and above it a fine waterfall. Cross Mill Bridge and pass in front of the old water-mill and around to the right to a gate above it. Pass through this and the gate beyond. The right wall drops away now and a splendid view of Dow Crag and Coniston Old Man opens up ahead. The path, a raised platform bordered by tree-stumps, follows the hedge round to a gate leading into a lane. Turn right along the lane and right again to reach the A5084 again near Torver village. Turn left here, and almost immediately right to walk through the village, passing a pub and the church.

Beyond the church, where the road swings right over a bridge, a lane fingerposted 'Walna Scar' climbs left. Follow this twisting lane, ignoring all openings to left or right. Eventually the tarmac ends and the track steepens and becomes stony underfoot. After passing through a gate near a ruin the left wall turns away and shortly, beyond a small quarry, a splendid view opens up ahead of Dow Crag and Coniston Old Man. Cross Tranearth Beck below the Lancashire Caving and Climbing Club Hut and continue along a stony lumpy path towards the spoil heaps of Banished Quarry. Pass through a gate and walk diagonally right to a gate signposted 'Walna Scar'. Beyond this turn right to cross a bridge over the Torver Beck. Climb the path through the spoil heaps to swing around to the right of a spectacular fenced-off flooded quarry with a beck cascading over its far rim. Continue up the path alongside the Torver Beck until a green path forks right. Turn right along this to shortly join the wider and stonier Walna Scar Road. Turn right along this track and just before a newish quarry road joins from the left look to your right for the small reedy depression grandiloquently christened Boo Tarn. Some 250 yards south-east, marked 'enclosure' on the 2½" map, is where several Bronze Age burial urns were unearthed in 1909. Along with the ashes of a child of around three years old was a charred fragment of cloth that was one of the earliest examples of woven British cloth. The urns are now in the Ruskin Museum in Coniston.

Return to the track and follow it down to the tarmac road and so back to Coniston.

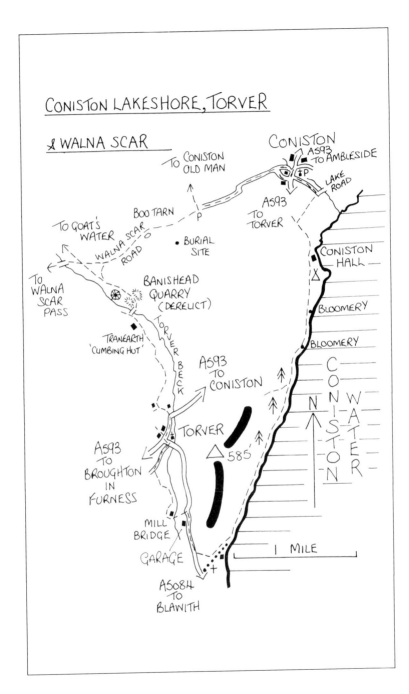

CONISTON LAKESHORE, TORVER

& WALNA SCAR

TO CONISTON OLD MAN

CONISTON
A593 TO AMBLESIDE

P

LAKE ROAD

A593 TO TORVER

BOO TARN

TO GOAT'S WATER

WALNA SCAR ROAD

P

BURIAL SITE

CONISTON HALL

TO WALNA SCAR PASS

BANISHEAD QUARRY (DERELICT)

BLOOMERY

BLOOMERY

TRANEARTH 'CLIMBING HUT'

TORVER BECK

A593 TO CONISTON

C O N I S T O N

N

W A T E R

A593 TO BROUGHTON IN FURNESS

TORVER

△ 585

MILL BRIDGE

GARAGE

1 MILE

A5084 TO BLAWITH

Hodge Close Quarries, Holme Fell and Ivy Crag

This superb short walk has infinite variety packed into its few miles. Hodge Close quarries may be a massive industrial scar but they are an integral part of Lakeland history. They have a dramatic beauty peculiarly their own and have become the playground of Lakeland's young 'tigers'. Holme Fell must be one of the most rugged of Lakeland's lower fells. The summit has a high-mountain feeling and the view from it is very fine.

Parking: From Coniston take the A593 Ambleside road for about three and a half miles, beyond its highest point, to where a forked minor road branches left, signposted 'High Park/Oxen Fell.' This road is also marked 'Cumbria Way' on the 2½" OS Map. Park on the verges. (GR329023).

TAKE the left hand fork of the minor road, past Low Oxen Farm, to a road junction. Turn right here to reach High Oxen Farm (note the date 1673 over the door). Go through the farmyard and through a gate leading on to a muddy track. After dropping into a hollow and crossing a beck the track climbs, twists and undulates whilst offering fine views. It eventually drops towards the buildings of Hodge Close, passing between a gate in a fence on your left and a small reedy tarn, with a ruin beyond, on your right. Shortly beyond these and before reaching the main buildings look for a narrow flight of slate steps leading down to your left. Descend these and the path through piled boulders below on to the floor of a huge quarry. Continue under a massive rock archway on to a rusting platform projecting over the deep green water flooding an even more spectacular quarry. Climbers may be in action on the vertiginous rocks to your left and divers in the translucent waters below you which plummet to a depth of one hundred feet.

Retrace your steps and upon emerging from the slate stairway turn left then left again to pass a cottage. Pots of tea are sometimes on sale here. Shortly you will emerge on to the dizzy rim of the flooded quarry. Continue around the rim to a gate. You will notice that the further depths of the quarry have been used by generations of Lakeland folk as a dumping ground for 'clapped-out jalopies' and 'owd baths'. Go through the gate to join and follow a path climbing gently rightwards through woodland alongside a wall. Pass through a gate. Presently the woods over the wall end and a

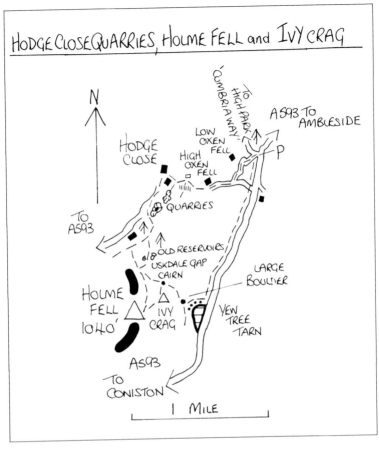

HODGE CLOSE QUARRIES, HOLME FELL and IVY CRAG

N

TO HIGH PARK CUMBRIA WAY

A593 TO AMBLESIDE

P

HODGE CLOSE

LOW OXEN FELL

HIGH OXEN FELL

QUARRIES

TO A593

OLD RESERVOIRS

USKDALE GAP

CAIRN

LARGE BOULDER

HOLME FELL 1040'

IVY CRAG

YEW TREE TARN

A593

TO CONISTON

1 MILE

row of cottages may be seen. Just before reaching a further gate look for a path climbing left. Follow this to a grassy crest from which you look over a heathery hollow to a rugged skyline. The prominent cairn marks the summit of Ivy Crag, with the higher summit of Holme Fell to its right. The gap below and to the left of Ivy Crag is Uskdale Gap. Bear right across the hollow to find and climb a path through the heather up onto the summit of Holme Fell which lies at the far end of a pronounced ridge. From the cairn there is a superb view down the length of Coniston Water. To the right of Coniston Water, Coniston Old Man and nearer Wetherlam dominate the skyline. From Wetherlam around to Black Crag there is a splendour of mountains – Crinkle Crags, Pike O'Blisco, Bowfell, Glaramara, the Langdale Pikes, Pavey Ark, High Raise, the gap of Dunmail Raise, Helvellyn and Fairfield. Return along the summit ridge before dropping right and heading towards Ivy

Crag. From its cairn the all-round view is equally spectacular. Yew Tree Tarn lies immediately below in the wooded depths of Yewdale, across which Tom Heights guards the popular and lovely Tarn Hows.

Head north from Ivy Crag and down into the Uskdale Gap. Turn right here and descend a steepish loose path towards Yew Tree Tarn. When a prominent boulder is reached turn left and follow a faint path to meet a wall coming in from your right. Turn left alongside the wall and follow it around to reach a stile. Cross the stile to follow a path veering left to a gate leading on to the A593. Ignore the gate and follow a faint path leftwards, climbing the fell alongside the wall. At the top of the hill a stile leads on to the road. Ignore it and continue alongside the wall/road. Climb a stile over a crossing wall and a further stile leading on to a minor road signposted 'High Oxen Farm'. Cross this, walk through trees and over a footbridge to cross a stile into a field. Continue alongside the wall to a stile which leads you back on to the road close to your car.

HAWKSHEAD

Medium Walk, 8 miles

Claife Heights

An enjoyable, nowhere strenuous, but oft-times boggy walk, through a mixture of woodland and open ground. The terrain gives varied views, highspots being the view from Wise Een Tarn of the Langdale Pikes and the 'bird's-eye' view on to Bell Isle and Bowness from Claife Heights. Bonuses are a chance of spotting deer, woodland birds, and wild fowl on the many tarns, named and un-named.

Parking: Hawkshead car park.

WALK back out of the car park and turn right. Turn left at the T-junction in the direction of 'Far Sawrey/Ferry'. Turn left again at the signpost 'Wray/Wray Castle'. Turn left at the next junction and walk through the hamlet of Colthouse, formerly a Quaker settlement. Follow the road up the hill to a gate on your right, opposite a drive entrance, signposted 'Public Bridleway – Claife Heights'.

Go through the gate and climb the worn path, alongside a fence, with a glimpse to your right of the Coniston Fells rising beyond Hawkshead. Climb further and Esthwaite Water will be glimpsed below. After passing a tarn in the woods to your right the trees and walls gradually close in before a gate is reached. (A roe deer once allowed itself to get trapped between me and this gate before bolting past me and down the path.)

Beyond the gate a sign on your right indicates 'Ferry/Sawrey' straight ahead. Descend to a forest road, where a 'Ferry' sign directs you to the right. The road descends then climbs left. As you crest the hill the road ahead can be seen to climb right. Follow it by all means, but a path climbing right hereabouts, between trees and a fence, provides a short cut, emerging onto the forest road above the bend. The road narrows into a path which passes to the right of a reedy un-named tarn. Pass through a waymarked gate and follow a wall onto open ground overlooking an un-named tarn on your left and larger Wise Een Tarn, 'tarn among the willow trees', to your right. North-westerly, and far beyond the glimmering waters of Wise Een, rise Bowfell's dark pyramid and the rugged, well-known outlines of the Langdale Pikes. The path passes below the dam of the smaller tarn, climbs over a rise, then drops down beside the rock-girt waters of Moss Eccles Tarn. A gate leads into a walled lane. Some distance down it look for a fork left, signposted 'Far Sawrey'. Descend to a footbridge over a beck, then join a tarmac drive and turn right eventually to emerge onto the B5285 in the hamlet of Far Sawrey, 'a muddy place'.

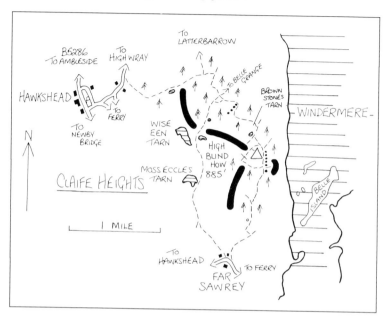

Turn left, passing the Sawrey Hotel, then turn left again, just past a telephone box, along a path signposted 'Public Bridleway/ Claife Heights'. This path eventually climbs right over a rise, passes through a gate and turns left up a walled path signposted 'Hawkshead'. At the top bear right, past a tiny tarn, before climbing between woods into an open area where the path forks. Descend right, following the 'Hawkshead' sign on the wall to your right. Soon the path climbs steeply up Low Pate Crag. Catch a glimpse of Windermere over your right shoulder. When the angle eases and the dark conifers close in look for a path leading through a gap in the wall to your right. Follow it on to a rocky ridge giving a superb 'bird's-eye' view of Belle Isle and Bowness. Return through the gap and turn right, shortly to reach a path fork with a 'Hawkshead' sign and white arrow pointing left. Climb left, following white marker posts, to reach the rock-crowned summit of High Pate Crag. Here, a 'Hawkshead' sign directs you right down a conifer tunnel, followed by a climb on to another rocky outcrop. Here, another 'Hawkshead' sign points you right down to a footbridge over a beck. Follow marker posts in a further climb to where a 'Viewpoint' sign directs you right on to the rocky summit of High Blind How. Return to the path and turn right, down on to a crossing path.

Variation: (This point can be reached more directly, should you wish to avoid the climbing, by going to the right of the 'Hawkshead' sign and white arrow, along a boggy path to the left of an old wall. Shortly after passing the opening of a conifer tunnel forking right you meet the white-waymarked path descending from High Blind How.)

Turn left and follow the marker posts to emerge on to a forest road. Turn right, signposted 'Hawkshead', and shortly pass a sign indicating 'Brown Stones Tarn' to your left. Shortly beyond this a 'Hawkshead' sign directs you left into the woods. White marker posts and waymarked rocks lead you through conifer aisles and tunnels. Soon after an old wall is seen in the trees to your left, a cairn and 'Hawkshead' sign, near a clearing, indicate a left turn. Go left eventually to emerge on to the bend of a forest road. Walk straight ahead along the road to rejoin your outward route where you took a 'short cut' right.

Blelham Tarn, Windermere
and Latterbarrow

A splendid walk through a variety of scenery. Lunch can be taken on the shore of Windermere, and the climax of the walk, the short climb up Latterbarrow, brings you one of the finest views in Lakeland.

Parking: Hawkshead village car park.

LEAVE the car park and turn left along the road. When the road swings left look for a lane, to the left of a high wall, over the road to your right. Go down this to see a 'Footpath' sign ahead. Follow the tarmac right, then left, around a white house where it ends. A path now continues ahead to reach a footbridge over a beck. Cross this and turn left to follow the beck for a short while before bearing right to a gate. Beyond this the path slants across a field to a stile. Beyond the stile the path forks, near a large boulder. Turn left to reach another stile at the end of a wall. The path now bears slightly right, with a barn above and to your right. To the left Coniston Old Man and Wetherlam can be seen rising above the lesser fells. A gate now leads into a narrow lane; turn left up this. Soon a gate will be seen on your right below a massive oak. Beyond the gate follow the path climbing up beside a fence. A further stile is crossed to reach the crest of the hill. A farm will be seen ahead and to your left. Beyond this rises the rounded shape of Red Screes, above Ambleside, with John Bell's Banner to its right and the Fairfield Fells to its left.

Go through a gate and follow the path to the left of a hummock to reach a road. Beyond the far wall Ambleside and the head of Windermere can be seen. Turn left between farm buildings and look for a gate on your right marked 'Footpath High Wray'. Pass through this and between walls to find a stile on your left. Ignore this and go through the gate ahead and follow the left-hand hedge to a gate and stile in the corner of the field below. Follow the marker posts over a rise, with the distant and graceful shapes of Froswick and Ill Bell beyond. Follow the posts down and across a culvert then up to a stile in the corner of the field. Cross this and follow the posts uphill to pass through a tree line. Continue beyond this to meet a wall. Turn left now and follow the wall to a gate in a corner.

Ahead you will now catch a glimpse of Blelham Tarn. Any strange objects seen on its surface are part of experiments conducted by the Freshwater Biological Association. Go through the gate and head downhill to a stile/gate in a field corner. This leads onto a farm lane; turn right and up to a road. Turn left here and follow the road down until it swings right. A signpost 'Footpath to Wray' will be seen on your left directing you onto a path passing in front of Hole House. Beyond the house a stile is crossed and the path follows a wall and fence, crosses a beck, bears left, and when Blelham Tarn is seen again, begins to bear right. Beyond Blelham Tarn you are looking straight into the heart of the Fairfield Horseshoe, a classic fell-walk. Another stile is crossed before the path drops down towards woods. Soon a finger-post directs you to the left to a gate between slate slabs. The path now swings right, around the base of a sloping field,to another gate. Follow the path towards a mound crowned by trees. Go to the left of this mound and into trees to meet a gate and a slate footbridge over a beck. Beyond the bridge head uphill with the fence/hedge to your right. Just after passing a gate in this fence the faint path heads into a wooded dip and swings round to the right to reach a gate leading onto a road. Marker posts hereabouts ease your navigation.

Turn left here and follow the road uphill to reach a church and the entrance to Wray Castle. A path to the right of the church is signposted 'Public Bridleway'. Follow this down until you see a stile on your left. This leads onto the grassy shores of High Wray Bay. A most pleasant spot for lunch, given the weather and lack of speedboats towing surfaced or submerged water-skiers. After lunch return over the stile and walk left until just beyond a boathouse and a stile another stile will be seen to your right. Cross this and follow the path uphill with a wall to your right. Pass between slate gate-posts and continue uphill. A look back across the lake sees the summit of Ill Bell to the right of Wansfell, and a glance over the wall to your right gives a fine view of the Langdale Pikes. Keeping the wall on your right brings you to a gate. Continue to follow the right wall, behind a house, to reach a stile in a corner which leads onto a drive. Turn right, through a gate, and onto a road. Turn left and walk up through the hamlet of High Wray. Pass a minor road on the left marked 'Ferry – Unit for Cars' and continue uphill until a sign 'National Trust, Base Camp' points across a cattle-grid to your left.

Cross the cattle-grid and follow a rough road to a junction at a National Trust sign 'Base Camp'. The left fork leads towards buildings in the woods. You take the right fork to a gate/stile. Beyond this the road begins to swing left, uphill. Look for a path here leading to the right to a stile in a fence in the trees. This path eventually crosses a beck, follows a fence for a while, then climbs upwards through the woods, eventually emerging into a more open area to reach a stile over a wall. Beyond this a further climb brings you to the summit of Latterbarrow and a superb view. The

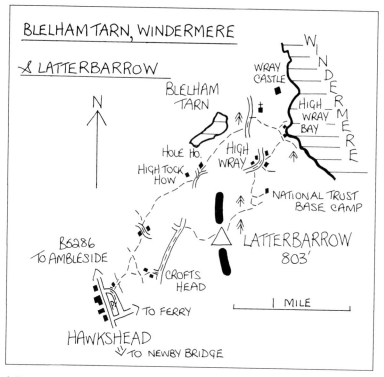

BLELHAM TARN, WINDERMERE

& LATTERBARROW

fells seen, both high and low, are too numerous to describe. The summit of Latterbarrow is a grand spot for the knowledgeable to air their knowledge and the less knowledgeable to get out their maps and attempt to orientate themselves.

For the descent head down in the general direction of Hawkshead. At the foot of the hill a path will be met which heads down to the right to a gate leading onto a road. Turn left down the road shortly passing another road on your right. Further down the road a lane runs down to your right towards houses, Crofts Head. Follow this. Look for a gate to the right of a garage in an opening on your left. Go through this and follow the path, bearing right, to a slate stile. Turn left beyond this and go past a forked ash tree. Esthwaite Water may be seen to your left here. The path now goes between rock outcrops before swinging right to another stile. Beyond this head downhill to a gate leading into a narrow lane. Turn right here then almost immediately left over a stile. Follow the path, bearing right around the foot of a hillock, and you will reach your outgoing route at the fork and boulder previously mentioned. Cross the stile and return by the same route.

LANGDALE

The Langdale Pikes via Dungeon Ghyll

The Langdale Pikes must be known to a high percentage of this country's population. People who have never set foot on a fellside must be familiar with the rugged skyline that has graced untold calenders, Christmas cards and book covers. They were the first mountains I ever climbed, some forty-odd years ago, and undoubtedly many walkers hold them in that same sentimental regard. The walk described below has some mild scrambling in its early stages but if you find yourself deterred by this it can be avoided. This scrambling however leads to two hidden waterfalls and a splendid rocky gorge.

Parking: In the free car-park, on the right, just beyond the entrance drive to the Stickle Barn-New Dungeon Ghyll Hotel complex. (GR 295065).

AT the lower end of the car park, above a gate, a path climbs right through the trees to a kissing-gate. Beyond it, turn left to another kissing-gate. Beyond this turn right and follow the wall, passing a seat, to reach another kissing-gate. Beyond this cross the Dungeon Ghyll and follow the well-worn path on its left bank. After a short climb a path will be seen slanting down to the right into the bed of the ghyll, and the entrance to the rocky shaft containing Dungeon Ghyll Force. Stepping carefully and depending upon the amount of water coming down it is possible to enter the gloomy rift and peer up at the roaring fall. Coleridge, himself an active and enthusiastic fell-walker, is reputed to have modelled the waterfall in his poem 'Kubla Khan' upon this Lakeland cascade. Indeed, in the late forties, a literary minded English rock-climber celebrated both this and his first ascent of a new hard climb on Pavey Ark by christening the climb 'Alph', after the 'sacred river' in the same poem.

Climb back out and continue up the path until yet another path slants down into the bed of the ghyll, above the force. Follow the beck bed, which may entail zig-zagging from bank to bank, until it turns right to meet another fine cascade and a rock pool. Scramble up either bank of the cascade and follow the beck into a rocky gorge. Follow its fascinating twists for a mile or so. There is some interesting scrambling and again a zig-zag course is necessary. Eventually a lovely high cascade, falling into a rocky basin, is reached. To the left a gully will be seen running into the fellside; scramble up this to reach easy ground. Now follow the beck above

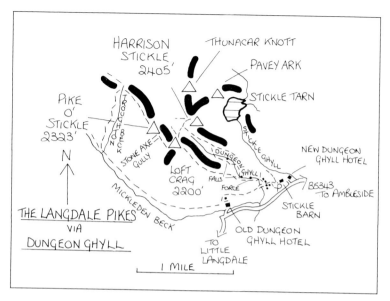

The Langdale Pikes via Dungeon Ghyll

the cascade. Loft Crag and Harrison Stickle now tower impressively ahead with the craggy crest of Pavey Ark thrusting up further to the right. Ahead the beck will be seen to disappear into another rocky gorge. A way can be made up this but the scrambling involved is more serious and I do not feel I should recommend it in a guide-book of this type.

It is possible that some readers of this booklet may have already been deterred from entering the lower gorge because of the 'scramble' up either bank of the first cascade. If this happens return downstream and climb back on to the original path. Follow this until the angle eases and Loft Crag and Harrison Stickle can be seen ahead. A walk to the right now should bring you back to the bank of the ghyll, above the high cascade and the gorge. Whichever way you arrive at this point now cross the beck and climb the obvious path on the far (right) bank. Follow this path which becomes more rocky and interesting as it traverses below the steep broken crags of Harrison Stickle and above the upper gorge of the Dungeon Ghyll. Eventually easier ground is reached and a junction with the 'tourist' route. Turn right along this and a short climb brings you to the summit of Harrison Stickle. The view is extensive and particularly fine towards Windermere. There is a fine 'birdseye' view of Stickle Tarn below and an interesting profile of Pavey Ark's climbing crag. To the west the Scafells and the 'hump' of Gable are predominant with the cocky thrust of Pike O'Stickle, your next objective, in the foreground. Descend back to and across the beck at the head of the gorge. A well-worn path will be seen heading directly towards Pike O'Stickle. If the day is clear however an interesting alternative, which requires little extra expenditure of energy, is to first climb the less obtrusive peak of Loft Crag. From it head towards Pike O'Stickle by following the edge of the crags. By looking down to the left a superb view will be seen of the north-west face of Gimmer Crag, where lie some of Lakeland's hardest rock-climbs. The original path is now joined at the foot of the summit rocks of Pike O'Stickle. To your left, at this point, an obvious gully drops steeply away.

This gully is known as Stone Axe Gully due to the discovery, in 1947, that a small square-cut cave in its right wall was a 'factory' for the production of Neolithic axe-heads. Since then other 'factories' have been uncovered on Harrison Stickle, Glaramara, Great End and Scafell Pike. Evidently these Neolithic fellsman were not only expert field geologists but capable of organising a system of production and distribution that saw Lakeland axe-heads exported to a wide area of the British Isles. The rock architecture on both sides of the gully is splendid and the cave lies about a third of the way down. To be honest, however, the descent is not recommended unless you are experienced in descending loose, shaly gullies that have become badly eroded by the slithery passage of thousands of axe-head seekers. If you have any doubts about your ability to cope with such terrain leave Stone Axe Gully alone and continue as follows.

Cross the head of the gully and scramble up to the summit of Pike O'Stickle for a breathtaking view of the notched skylines of Bowfell and Crinkle Crags across the airy gulf of Mickleden. Descend the summit rocks and head north-westerly along a path following the rim of the fell. This eventually descends into the hollow at the head of Troughton Beck, which it crosses before swinging sharply left to reach the rim of Mart Crag. From here it descends in steepish zig-zags eventually to join the main Langdale-Rosset Gill track on the floor of Mickleden. Now turn left along this track. When the gate at the rear of the Old Dungeon Ghyll Hotel is approached bear left up the fellside to a higher gate. Pass through this into a walled lane which passes behind a white house standing above the hotel. Follow this lane eventually to cross a footbridge over the Dungeon Ghyll and rejoin your outward route.

Lingmoor and Side Pike via Blea Tarn

A superb short walk taking in a variety of terrain and scenery and starting and finishing at a lovely picnic spot, with the possible chance of a close-up of rock-climbers in action. An excellent walk for introducing children to the hills with a promise of a paddle or swim in the tarn and a picnic by its shores at the end.

Parking: In the car-park, near Blea Tarn, on the road connecting Great Langdale with Little Langdale. (GR 296044).

LEAVE the car park, turn right, and walk up the road. Shortly after the wall on your right turns away look for a faint path slanting up the fellside. Climb this to join a more well-worn path on the right bank of the gill spilling down towards Blea Tarn House. Turn right up this path. Pause at your leisure, for the prospect behind you is worth any excuse for a 'breather'. The Langdale Pikes, towering above the craggy cone of Side Pike, dominate of course. Bowfell, five hundred feet higher and the true king of Langdale's mountains, stands back and you only get a taste of the mighty rampart it forms, with Crinkle Crags, around the dalehead. Below your toe-caps gleams Blea Tarn, a delight yet to come. Beyond the depths of Little Langdale rise Wetherlam, Swirl How, and Great Carrs, northern outliers of the Coniston Fells.

Eventually your path moves left, through some splendid pines, into the head of the gill to a stile. Cross the stile and turn left to climb steeply alongside the wall/fence to shortly reach a stile in a fence leading to the large cairn crowning aptly named Lingmoor, 'the fell of the heather, or ling'. The 2½″ map says 'Brown Howe' but Wainright, Griffin, a million fellwalkers, and me, call it 'Lingmoor'. Windermere is now added to the view and for the collector of scenic curiosities, given a clear day, Blackpool Tower may be picked out to the left of Wetherlam (the furthest left of the Coniston Fells).

Descend beyond the cairn following the path alongside the wall/fence crowning the fell, the Langdale Pikes looking more magnificent with every onward step. Below, to your right, lies unpublicised and rarely visited Lingmoor Tarn. Yet I have seen its surface sown with the lovely Bogbean, and the Pikes, blazoned in Autumn colours, mirrored pin-sharp there. After a rocky step, awkward when slimy or icy, a stile transfers you across the fence/wall. Now follow the wall towards the increasingly forbidding crags of Side Pike. Don't worry, all will be revealed! Cross the stile below the

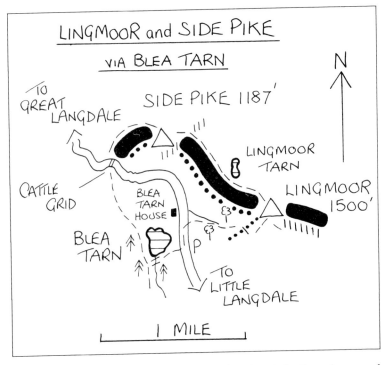

LINGMOOR and SIDE PIKE

VIA BLEA TARN

N

SIDE PIKE 1187'

TO GREAT LANGDALE

LINGMOOR TARN

CATTLE GRID

BLEA TARN HOUSE

LINGMOOR 1500'

BLEA TARN

P

TO LITTLE LANGDALE

1 MILE

crag and follow a path which climbs right, then left, then down and round to a ledge apparently blocked by a rock pinnacle. Pushing your rucksack before you, squeeze behind the pinnacle onto the ledge beyond. It's good fun and much easier than it looks. I've encouraged several dubious and 'pleasantly plump' ladies and gentlemen safely through. Ancient climbing guidebooks used to call such features a 'Fat Man's Agony'. Follow the ledge around a corner and climb a path forking right to eventually meet an old wall and a wider path. Turn right and follow this to reach the summit of Side Pike. The Pikes look even more impressive from here. Retrace your steps and follow the path alongside the wall down to a stone memorial bench and a stile leading onto the road.

Cross the road, go left through a gap in a wall and down towards Blea Tarn. A tunnel of rhododendrons leads you along the western shore then turn left over a footbridge onto the open, grassy south shore. Pause here and look with pride at the rugged skyline you have traversed, and the real and water-mirrored array of Pike O'Stickle, Loft Crag, Harrison Stickle, and Pavey Ark. (Julie Walters and friends 'skinny-dipped' here in the film 'She'll Be Wearing Pink Pyjamas'). Your car is nearby so you have time to follow suit!

The Elterwater Round

A fine all-weather walk full of interest. It holds two rivers, two fine waterfalls, a unique slate gallery, a minor lake, a huge man-made cavern, and numerous picnic and bathing places in its few miles.

Parking: The car-park in Elterwater village, opposite the Brittania Inn.

GO through the gate signposted 'Riverside Walk to Skelwith Bridge'. The path follows the river-bank then enters the wood bordering Elterwater, 'the swan lake'. Beyond the woods it emerges into open fields again before reaching a gate leading into the gorge containing Skelwith Force. 'Skelwith', roughly translated, means 'the noisy water near a wood, or ford'. The cascade is a fine one, particularly in spate, and bridges lead out onto the rocks for a closer look. After inspecting the falls continue along the river bank, passing through the buildings of the slateworks, to reach Kirkstone Slate Galleries, which are open seven days a week.

After visiting the galleries walk down the drive to Skelwith Bridge. Cross the bridge and follow the road round the sharp corner and up the hill to reach a signpost indicating 'Colwith Bridge', to the right. Turn into the access lane where, after a short walk, a gate signposted 'Colwith Bridge' will be seen on the left. Beyond this the path climbs over a wooded hill to meet a grassy drive coming in from the road on the left. From this point Wetherlam can be seen rising to the left of the trees ahead whilst to their right can be seen Pike O'Blisco and the triple-peaked Crinkle Crags. Turn right along the drive and follow it down past a farmhouse. Ahead, across a field, will be seen a row of caravans. Follow the path heading towards these, looking to the right for a distant view of Seat Sandal and Fairfield, with Dollywaggon Pike filling the gap of Grisedale Hause between them.

Pass through a gate and climb up past the caravans to reach a signpost indicating 'Colwith' is to the left. Walk through a farmyard to where 'public footpath' is indicated in a gap between two buildings. Beyond the gap head down across the grass; there is a sign 'Colwith' in the hedge to your right. A stile is now reached from which a fine view of the Langdale Pikes can be seen. The path now leads down to a stile in the end of a wall. Beyond this a narrow passage leads on to a drive on the other side of which is a kissing-gate. Pass through the gate and follow the path down the field to a stile at the edge of a wood. Beyond this the path runs high above the river before dropping down to the water's edge and

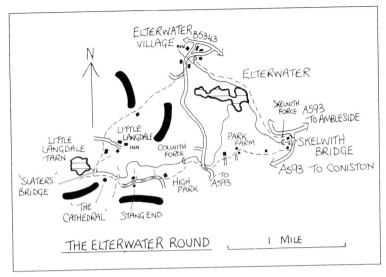

THE ELTERWATER ROUND   1 MILE

yet another stile. Now cross over a field to a stile leading on to a road. Turn right along the road but before reaching the bridge (Colwith Bridge), a stile will be seen on the left, signposted 'Public Footpath'. Beyond this stile the path forks. Take the lower right fork, alongside the river, to eventually reach a rocky point overlooking Colwith Force, to my mind the superior of the two waterfalls. 'Colwith' means the 'charcoal wood'.

To continue, follow the path leading above the falls and along the river to reach a stile. Beyond this the path begins to climb up through the woods, passing one particularly fine beech tree, to reach a gate. Pass through this and walk alongside a wall to reach another gate from where there is a superb view of Bowfell framed between Pike O'Blisco and Lingmoor. Pass through this gate to reach High Park Farm and through the farmyard to reach a road. Now turn right down the road to reach the cottages at Stang End.

Continue down the road which crosses a bridge over a beck before swinging around a wooded hill to a ford and footbridge over the River Brathay. Walk left, past the footbridge, following the path above and alongside the river. Keep your eyes open for a gate on your left beyond which a path climbs through a slate spoil-heap. Go through the gate, climb left, then right, to a hut with a National Trust emblem on its door.

Behind the hut is a rock fissure crowned by a slate arch. Pass under the arch and follow the fissure, do not be deterred by the low wet tunnel ahead, and continue until a hidden opening on the left leads to a dramatic view of a huge man-made cavern, 'The Cathedral', supported by a central leaning pillar. (**Since writing**

32

this account I have visited this spot to find there has been a heavy rockfall into the fissure, and in order to view the cavern you have to climb over the fall. The cavern is a magnificent sight but obviously there is some danger and it is up to each individual to decide if the risk is warranted). Should you wish to venture into 'The Cathedral' return past the hut to the lower terrace. A few yards along it you will see a tunnel on your right with a glimpse of 'The Cathedral' at its far end. The tunnel is wet underfoot but enterprising explorers have positioned 'stepping stones' which enable you to avoid most of the water. Return the same way or walk past the leaning pillar and pass through a short tunnel. Now climb the 'scrambly' path which eventually leads you out on to the rim of the quarry. Turn right and down to reach the hut once more.

Return down through the gate then walk left to where a kissing-gate in the wall on your right leads down to the lovely packhorse Slaters Bridge. This is a lovely spot for a picnic and there are fine bathing pools above and below the bridge. Cross the bridge and follow the path running up alongside the wall to reach a gate leading into a lane. There is a fine view back across Little Langdale Tarn towards Wetherlam, Great Carrs, and the twisting road leading up to Wrynose Pass. Turn left along the lane to meet the road. Go left along this a little way before turning right up a lane marked 'Unfit for Cars'. After some climbing the lane eventually descends through woods to meet a road. Turn right down this and soon Elterwater village is entered near to the car-park.

AMBLESIDE

Fell Walk, 7 miles

Red Screes via Scandale

An excellent fell-walk of its type. Nowhere really strenuous and giving a superb variety of scenery.

Parking: In one of Ambleside's car-parks.

WALK up the street (North Road), behind the shops facing the old Bus Station and Gaynors shop, to its junction with Smithy Brow, above the Golden Rule pub. Climb right to shortly see a 'High Sweden Bridge Lane' sign on your left. Climb left up this lane, ignoring a left fork 'Low Sweden Bridge', to where the tarmac ends at a gate. Beyond the gate the lane narrows, between drystone walls, and becomes rough underfoot. Already there is a fine view over the left-hand wall, down into the Rothay valley and across to Loughrigg and beyond it to the Langdale and Coniston fells. The lane twists and climbs steadily through woods before eventually emerging into the high valley of Scandale. The path forks here with the left-hand path crossing Scandale Beck by a packhorse bridge (High Sweden Bridge), before climbing up to the crest of the Low Pike to High Pike ridge. This ridge is the tip of the eastern horn of the popular Fairfield Horseshoe walk.

Your way lies straight ahead, however, up Scandale – 'the short dale'. Red Screes is the rounded fell to the right and the saddle straight ahead is Scandale Pass, with the twin-peaks of Little Hart Crag peering cockily over it. A 'green' road can be seen running directly up the floor of the U-shaped valley to end a few hundred feet below the crest of the pass. It is not, as it might appear, a drove road but a kind of funnel built in order to move sheep quickly down the fells. Many of Lakeland's myriad walls were built in the period 1795-1820. A growing population created a demand for food and the successive wars with France doubled the price of wool. Both these causes led to an increase in the enclosure of formerly barren land. The history of Lakeland wall-building must be worth a treatise in itself. Many walls go back long before the period mentioned. A collapsed dike on Nab Scar, above Rydal, can be dated 1277. A sheep boundary in Ling Cove, Eskdale, can be dated 1290, and a wall on Red Screes, above Kirkstone Pass, can be dated 1680. Many can be almost regarded as works of art. The wall running along the Low Pike-Dove Crag ridge, above to your left, is continuous for two miles.

The 'funnel' gives pleasant walking and when it ends a good path leads, a little more steeply, up to a stile in the wall running across the crest of Scandale Pass. The valley beyond is called Caiston Glen and the path continues down this and eventually arrives at Patterdale. The steep scree-covered slopes of John Bell's Banner can be seen, above the Kirkstone road, and beyond that the more distant High Street range. To the left is the fine profile of the previously mentioned Little Hart Crag. This is a fine rocky peak apparently rarely climbed. For those with energy to spare it is worth the detour. Simply follow the wall until it veers left, then leave it and head for the base of the rocks. There is a good view from the summit of Dovedale and Brotherswater.

Returning to Scandale Pass, or if you have not left it, attack Red Screes by following the path running alongside the wall. After crossing a mossy slab the angle steepens a little before a crossing wall is met. Looking down to the left from this section there is a fine view of Brotherswater. Leave the walls now and head easterly, across gradually easing grass slopes, to reach the trig point near a shallow tarn. The trig point is perched on the edge of steep screes and shattered crags giving a bird's-eye view down to Brotherswater. The all-round view is extensive and varied and happy moments could be spent identifying the various fells and lakes.

For the descent head south-westerly, following the path that runs above the eastern edge of the fell. This shortly brings you above the corrie whose sanguine crags and screes give the mountain its name. (On some maps the mountain is called 'Kilnshaw Chimney' but this is actually a natural rock-feature in the crags above Kirkstone). From here there is an exhilarating bird's-eye view of the Kirkstone Pass Inn. Continue past the cairn on Raven Crag, with island-studded Windermere always before your eyes. Eventually a stile over a wall leads into another 'funnel' which twists down to a gate leading out on to the road above 'The Struggle'. Turn right here and Ambleside is shortly reached.

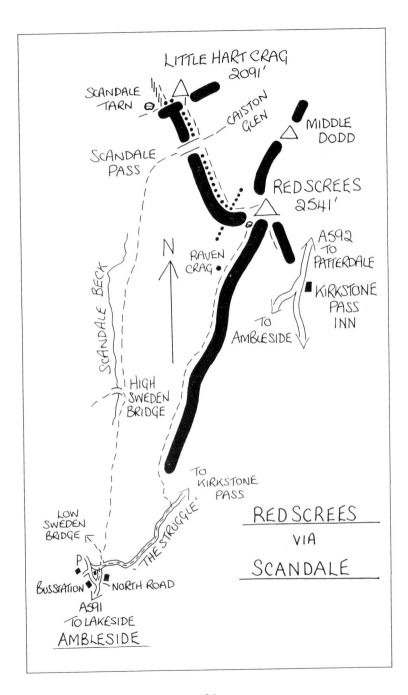

Stock Ghyll and the
High Lanes of Wansfell

This walk is full of variety. The climb up Wansfell requires 'a bit of puff' but the views give ample excuse to pause for a breather and are even finer from the summit. The 'high lanes' are a delight. A walk along them evokes a past Lakeland and it is not hard to imagine a jingling pack-horse train, a pair of moleskin-clad itinerant quarry-men, or a stovepipe-hatted poet and his crinolined entourage, around the next corner. All this plus some fine cascades, a 16th century house of historic interest and a constantly changing variety of scenery makes six miles seem a delightful stroll.

Parking: As for Walk 10.

IN AMBLESIDE, pass between the Market Hall (now a restaurant) and a bank and turn left to follow the lane leading behind the *Salutation Hotel.* Shortly, fork left through a gate into Stock Gill Park. The wooded cascades of Stock Gill Force are worth the diversion, especially if in spate. Paths climb up either bank and there are various viewing points. Just below the head of the falls, in a wall to your right, there is a rusty turnstile. After exploring the falls pass through this on to the lane beyond. This turnstile is a relic of the days when the cascades were privately owned and could only be visited upon payment of a fee. It also vividly recalls to me a school-trip to the Lakes aeons ago.

Turn left to cross over a cattlegrid. From here Red Screes dominates the skyline with the sanguine rocks of the huge corrie below the summit giving vivid testimony to the aptness of its name. A few hundred yards beyond the cattle-grid, near a green hut, a stile in the wall on the right is signposted 'Wansfell' and 'Troutbeck'. Cross the stile and ascend the well-worn path climbing steeply up to the obvious rocky knoll on the skyline above. It's a strenuous climb but as stated the views behind your back give every excuse for a halt. The Rothay valley twists away below your feet, guarded on the right by Fairfield and its satellite peaks and on the left by the hummocky plateau of Loughrigg, whilst beyond Loughrigg there is a dramatic skyline stretching from Coniston Old Man to Ullscarf. Rydal Water graces the head of the valley with just a glint of Grasmere peering around the foot of Nab Scar.

The rocky knoll is not the true summit, which lies a few yards beyond over a stile. The few steps to the top bring a sudden and

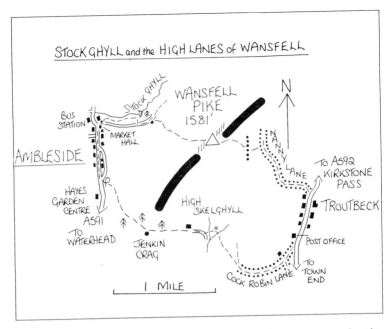

superb view down the gleaming length of Windermere. In the opposite direction the notch of Kirkstone Pass is obvious with the volcano-like summit of Angle Tarn Pike, above Patterdale, peeking over it. Working right from the pass are John Bell's Banner, Thornthwaite Crag, with its splendid chimney-like cairn, followed by the shapely cones of Froswick and Ill Bell, and the more prosaic Yoke which leads down to the Garburn Pass. Harter Fell (Mardale) peers over the dip between Thornthwaite Crag and Froswick and also, if the light is right, the spirals of the Roman military road can be seen descending from this same dip. Without an early form of it, apparently 'Wansfell' cannot be interpreted except that the first element may be a personal name.

Descend easterly, along a cairned path, over easy ground, to a gate in a wall. Shortly beyond this another gate leads into Nanny Lane. Turn right and follow this lane which goes most pleasantly down to the village of Troutbeck. Across the other side of the valley the walled lane that leads up to Garburn Pass can be seen slanting across the fellside. Below it is the very popular Lime Fitts Caravan and Camping Site. Upon reaching the road turn right and walk through the village until, just beyond a post-box in a wall, another walled lane forks upwards to the right, signposted 'Bridleway to Ambleside'. (Town End, a 16th century Lakeland dwelling house now owned by the National Trust, lies a short detour down the road should you wish to visit it).

Climb the walled Cock Robin Lane, which gradually levels and swings right. It's delightful walking, above a gleaming Windermere and with Wetherlam, Harrison Stickle, and their like, crowding into view around every corner. A final corner brings Wansfell Pike looming above. A gate/stile signposted 'Ambleside/Jenkin Crag', to your left, leads you gradually down, across a beck and past a ruin, to a tarmac road. Turn right up the tarmac to High Skelghyll Farm. Pass through the yard, and in front of the farmhouse, to a gate leading on to a path descending into Skelghyll Wood. Shortly after entering the wood a sign 'Jenkin Crag' will be seen on your left. Walk out on to its rocky summit for an enchanting view over Windermere and the humped and lovely fells encircling it. Return to the path and twist down through the woods. (We've spotted a fox hereabouts so keep your eyes open). The path leads onto a tarmac strip which leads down to a road behind a car-park. Cross the car-park to reach Lake Road and follow it back into Ambleside.

Todd Crag and Rydal Park

For me this walk is worth any effort involved simply for the bird's-eye view of the remains of the Roman fort at Waterhead. If however history is not your bent the views are, naturally in Lakeland, superb. There are literary associations and Rydal Cave is impressive; and after the initial climb is achieved the expenditure of energy required is slight.

Parking: As for Walks 10 and 11.

LEAVE Ambleside by Compston Road (behind the Bus Station). A few hundred yards down this road turn right into Vicarage Road, signposted 'Rydal Park/Loughrigg'. Walk through Rydal Park and cross the River Rothay by a hump-backed bridge to join a road. Turn right, across a cattle grid, then almost immediately left, across another cattle grid, on to a tarmac bridleway signposted 'Loughrigg'. Climb this until at a sharp right turn, above the buildings at 'Brow Head', a metal stile signposted 'Clappersgate' will be seen on your left. Cross this and walk left to pass through a gap in a slate fence. Paths climb to the right and left of the wooded hillock above you. Climb the left-hand path, heading towards a rocky summit. Cross its cairned top through a gap in a wall. Cross the next summit by a stile over a wall, then a third summit to reach the rocky rounded fourth, and arguably highest, summit of Todd Crag.

The 'bird's-eye' view over Windermere is breathtaking. My eyes always wander, however, to the ruins of 'Galava', the Roman fort, on its promontory by the mouth of the Rothay. You're gazing upon the archetypal plan of a military fort that remained unchanged for centuries and was planted upon conquered soil from Persia to Perthshire. Roman sentries may have looked up and seen a Brigante war-party poised, like Apaches in a John Wayne film, on the very rocks upon which you are standing.

Return into the dip between the last two summits and turn down left. Climb over a rise and past a small tarn. Climb again to pass to the right of larger Lily Tarn. Shortly, the path veers left to pass alongside a wall then down to a gate in a fence. Beyond this, cross a path and climb straight over the hillock ahead into a dip with a tiny tarn to your left. Look down to your right to spot a wall. Head for the curving wall corner, crossing en-route a path issuing from a gate. (Should you wish to return directly to Ambleside follow this path through the gate). Near the wall corner stepping stones cross

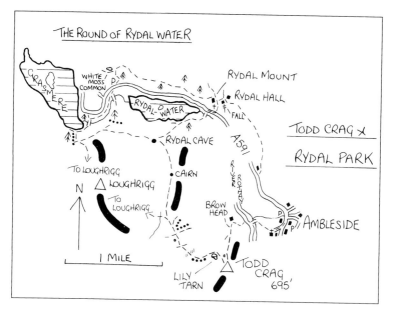

THE ROUND OF RYDAL WATER

RYDAL MOUNT
RYDAL HALL
WHITE MOSS COMMON
RYDAL WATER
GRASMERE
FALL
TODD CRAG x
RYDAL PARK
RYDAL CAVE
A591
TO LOUGHRIGG
CAIRN
N
LOUGHRIGG
TO LOUGHRIGG
RIVER ROTHAY
BROW HEAD
AMBLESIDE
P
P
1 MILE
LILY TARN
TODD CRAG 695'

a boggy patch. Just beyond, the path crosses rocks. Fork left here up a path leading to another fork. Fork right now and climb gradually to reach a cairn. Go beyond the cairn and down to eventually pass through an area of dwarf juniper. Dwarf juniper was particularly used for the production of charcoal for Lakeland's now-defunct gunpowder industry. Soon Rydal Water will be seen below with Helm Crag towering impressively beyond. Look over your left shoulder to spot a fine waterfall.

Your path emerges on to a rough track near a beck. (If you have not already visited Rydal Cave (described in Walk 13), climb left up the track, past a quarry/cave guarded by a rock pinnacle, to reach it. After exploring the cave return down the track). If you already have visited Rydal Cave then turn right down the rough track keeping your eyes open for a path dropping down the steep bank on your left, past a seat, to a metal gate in a wall just above the lakeshore. Go through this gate and follow a wooded path to a footbridge over the Rothay. (I've seen an otter hereabouts). Cross the bridge and climb up on to the A591. Turn right, then shortly left up the lane leading to Rydal Mount. Look for a 'Public Footpath' sign on your right, above the upper entrance to Rydal Hall. You might find the 'Tea Shop' sign below it more stimulating! Follow the signs between the buildings and over a bridge spanning the Rydal Beck. After passing the last building on your right, turn right and descend steps for a look at a splendid waterfall. Climb back and follow the fenced path through the grounds of Rydal

41

Hall. Etched on the skyline to your right are the heights you have just 'bagged'. Ornamental gates lead onto the A591 and so back to Ambleside.

RYDAL

The Round of Rydal Water

This delightful and amiable walk can be accomplished in a couple of hours but wisely you will linger over it. You can then appreciate the literary associations, the scenery, and the countless opportunities this walk gives to picnic, swim, paddle, bird-watch, sketch, or whatever takes your fancy.

Parking: In the car-park, through a log archway, in the derelict quarry below White Moss Common, on the northern verge of the A591. (GR 348065).

CROSS the A591 and follow the path down on to the banks of the Rothay. Turn right, and ignoring the bridge over the river, pass through a gate. Follow the path alongside the river to a gate. Beyond it, paths fork. Take the left fork over a rise and down to a footbridge over the river. Cross this bridge and turn right on to the pebbly beach which offers a fine prospect of Grasmere and its enfolding fells. Walk to the far end of the beach which is a lovely spot for a picnic and/ or swim. Don't go through the gate but climb steeply left up a rough path between a wall and a beck, to eventually emerge on to Loughrigg Terrace near a gate. Turn left along the terrace which is fortuitously provided with benches upon which you may regain your breath.

At the far end of the terrace take the path forking right which traverses across the fellside to a wooden bench. Climb above the bench to the huge, derelict quarry known as Rydal Cave, its entrance guarded by a dark, still pool of unfathomable water. Looking out, the jagged arch of the cave mouth curving over pool, larches, birches, far fellside and reflections thereof, forms a dramatic composition irresistible to photographers. Though you will probably be dissatisfied with your results, try it, we all do every time we visit!

After exploring the cave follow the track down past another quarry/cave guarded by a rock pinnacle. Continue down the track looking for a path descending the steep bank to your left, past a seat to a metal gate in a wall near the lake edge. Go through the gate and follow a wooded path to reach a footbridge over the Rothay just below where it empties from Rydal Water. After crossing the bridge a short climb brings you out on to the A591. Turn right here and follow the road until opposite the lane leading up to Rydal Mount.

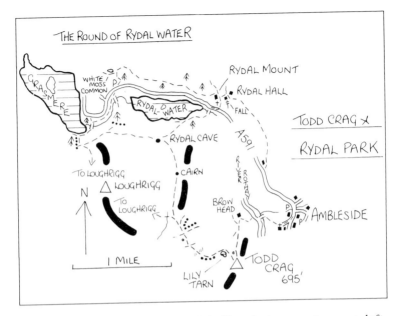

THE ROUND OF RYDAL WATER

Walk up the lane until Rydal Church is seen to your left. Wordsworth worshipped here, indeed he had a hand in choosing the site, and apparently often vociferously disparaged a sermon from the vantage-point of his front pew. If the daffodils are in bloom go through the churchyard into the little wood beyond. This is 'Dora's Field'. The flowers here were planted by the poet in memory of his daughter. After visiting the church continue up the lane to reach Rydal Mount. This was the poet's home for the last period of his life and he died here in 1850. The house is open to the public.

After visiting, or not, continue steeply on to where a narrow lane, signposted 'Public Bridleway/Grasmere', forks left above Rydal Mount. Go through a gate and follow the path which twists and undulates across the wooded south flank of Nab Scar. The trees part periodically, giving lovely views of Rydal Water. 'The dale where rye was grown' is the interpretation of 'Rydal'. Eventually, near a small reedy tarn, the end of a tarmac road is reached. Wordsworth is reputed to have skated on the frozen waters of this tarn. We once disturbed a heron fishing here, and have seen deer on the fellside opposite. Turn left here down a stony path to reach the carpark.

If you have energy to spare, before turning down the stony path, climb the fellside opposite the tarn on to the summit of White Moss Common for a lovely view over Rydal Water and Grasmere.

GRASMERE

Walk 14

Medium Walk, 3½ miles

Allcock Tarn

A pleasant walk combining scenic beauty with literary associations. This is a good walk for children. I always found the promise of a picnic near water a remarkable incentive to my children.

Parking: Grasmere village car-parks.

LEAVE Grasmere village by the road heading towards Ambleside. Upon reaching the junction with the main-road (Keswick to Ambleside A591), cross this and follow the minor road leading to Wordsworth's Dove Cottage. Wordsworth addicts may be tempted to visit. I only tried once and my entrance was firmly blocked by a cohort of matronly ladies from Milwaukee. After a short climb the road forks, signposted 'Rydal' to the right, and 'No Through Road For Motor Vehicles' to the left. Take the left-hand fork and after another short climb, a path signposted 'Footpath To Allcock Tarn' will be seen bearing left near a seat. Follow this to a gate where the path forks. Ignore the path branching up to the right, alongside the wall, and go through the gate. The path now climbs up through a tunnel of trees before emerging on to more open ground.

There is a bird's-eye view here down on to Grasmere, lake and village. Across the valley Helm Crag (The Lion and The Lamb) is predominant and beyond it Far Easedale leads up to the saddle of Greenup Edge, with High Raise and Ullscarf rising to the left and right of this. To the left of High Raise, the Langdale Pikes, Bowfell, Crinkle Crags, Pike O'Blisco and the Coniston Fells all reveal more of themselves as height is gained. To the right of Helm Crag bulky Steel Fell stands guard over the A591 and Dunmail Raise. The path now winds pleasantly upwards passing a little fish-pond overhung by larch trees. Eventually the path forks, the right fork leading up to an iron-gate in a walled lane, whilst the left fork slants through bracken towards a stand of trees. Climb the left fork, pass through a gate in a wall, and climb steeply up through a stand of trees. Move left across a beck before climbing steeply again to reach the rocky summit of Grey Crag. Sunk amongst these rocks you will see a metal tube. On Grasmere Sports day a flag is planted here and runners in the Fell Race toil up the steep fellside below you, round the flag and plunge recklessly downhill.

A short walk beyond leads to a gap in a wall and the banks of Allcock Tarn. The grassy banks of this lovely but somewhat austere tarn make a delightful picnic spot. Above the tarn rise the rock-strewn slopes of Heron Pike. Windermere can be seen to the south, with Morecambe Bay beyond if it is particularly clear, whilst to the west all the fells previously mentioned are spread in finer detail.

To descend follow the path along the edge of the tarn towards a rocky gap. A National Trust sign is reached, near a metal stile. Beyond the stile the path passes through a gap before beginning to swing left and downwards. The valley below is Greenhead Gill, the scene of Wordsworth's 'Michael', and there is an impressive view to the right up the upper reaches of it, dominated by the rounded summit of Great Rigg.

The zig-zag path drops steeply down into the bed of the gill. A bridge-like structure across the stream carries the Thirlmere-Manchester pipeline. The descent ends at a footbridge; cross it then turn left through a gate into a narrow lane. Follow this down to a minor road. A turn left here soon brings you down to the A591 near the *Swan Hotel*. Cross this to the road opposite which leads back into Grasmere village.

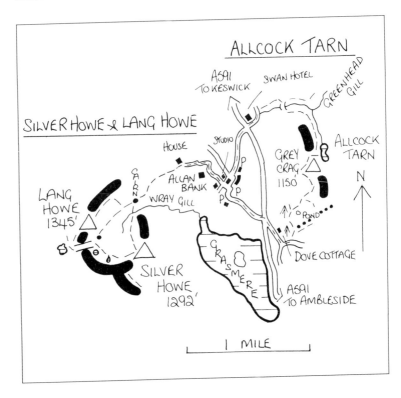

Silver Howe and Lang Howe

Looking across Grasmere from the A591 or up from Grasmere
village, Silver Howe dominates. Its apparent isolation and moun-
tainous outline make it appear much higher than its modest height
of around twelve hundred feet. The combined ascent of these two
modest fells nevertheless gives superb views and has a high mountain
air about it.

Parking: As for Walk 14, in Grasmere village.

LEAVE Grasmere by the lane to the left (as you face it) of
W. Heaton Cooper's Studio. Go through the gateposts and up the
drive to Allan Bank. When it was built Wordsworth called it a
'temple of abomination' and declared it would ruin the character
of the Vale of Grasmere. Years later with a growing family to
house, he was forced to eat his words and rent it for a while.

Just below the house the drive forks. A narrower drive bears
right and a small sign indicates 'Path' that way. This drive steepens
and gradually swings to the left. To your right there is a fine view of
Helm Crag, Dunmail Raise and Seat Sandal. Just before reaching
a white house a small sign indicates 'Silver Howe' to the left. Pass
through a gate and follow the path up into a sunken lane. This
leads up to a stile and beyond it to the open fell. The path now
steepens, with a wall to its left. When the wall falls back the angle
eases and the path winds through stunted juniper bushes to reach
two cairns. Here the path forks. Now follow the left-hand path
which shortly comes out above the ravine of Wray Gill. Shortly, it
forks again with the left-hand path dropping down into the bed of
the gill. Follow this path which, after crossing the gill, climbs up to
the right of a scree covered hillock. When it levels out Silver Howe
can be seen ahead, the left-hand and highest point on a hummocky
ridge. Below, to the right, is a boggy basin and beyond that is the
craggy outline of Lang Howe. A cairned and well-worn path leads
towards Silver Howe finishing with a short steep climb.

There is an extensive view down upon Grasmere and Rydal
Water, and towards the south and west. For the descent head
westerly (or to your right as you climbed up to the summit), and
down into a hollow to meet a path which runs across the head of
the boggy basin, in the direction of Lang Howe. Turn right and
follow this, passing eventually to the right of a small tarn choked
with plant life. Lang Howe looms quite impressively ahead. At its
foot a cairn will be met and a junction of paths and to the left

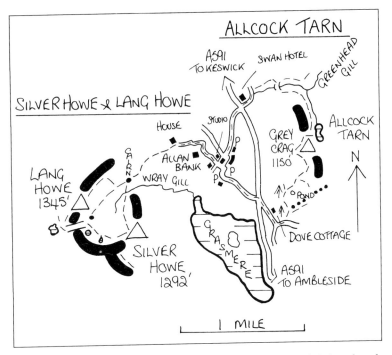

ALLCOCK TARN

SILVER HOWE & LANG HOWE

A591 TO KESWICK — SWAN HOTEL — GREENHEAD GILL

STUDIO — HOUSE — GREY CRAG 1150 — ALLCOCK TARN

CAIRN — ALLAN BANK — WRAY GILL — POND — DOVE COTTAGE

LANG HOWE 1345'

SILVER HOWE 1292'

GRASMERE

A591 TO AMBLESIDE

N

1 MILE

another, and slightly larger, tarn will be seen. Take the left-hand path and climb up to a saddle graced with a further cairn. Below this will be seen a yet larger plant-choked tarn. The eye will go beyond this however to a superb view of the fells gracing the head of Langdale. Framed between the striking silhouettes of Side Pike and Harrison Stickle are Pike O'Blisco, Crinkle Crags and Bowfell, all displaying their rugged architecture of crag and gill. Now scramble up grass to reach the rounded summit of Lang Howe. The summit has an air of isolation which is remarkable when you consider the popularity of Silver Howe, barely half a mile away, and the network of popular paths surrounding it. It is this charm, combined with its rugged outline from the Silver Howe approach, that gives this walk its higher mountain aspect.

For the descent either return to the second cairn, walk back over the saddle and down to the first cairn, then turn left here and follow the path descending down the left-hand side of the basin under Lang Howe, or follow the crest of Lang Howe for a little way before dropping, right, down grassy slopes to join the same path. This path eventually joins the ascending path on the banks of the Wray Gill. The return to Grasmere village from this point is now simply a reversal of the ascent. 'Howe' or 'how' originally meant a knoll or hillock but was later applied to quite large hills. It sometimes referred to actual or reputed grave mounds.

The Greenburn Horseshoe

Greenburn is surprisingly unfrequented despite its proximity to Grasmere. A round of its enfolding fells gives a delightful walk that is nowhere arduous once the initial climb up Steel Fell is overcome. As Lakeland fells go Steel Fell and Helm Crag are low in stature but high in quality. The views over Thirlmere and the Vale of Grasmere are particularly fine.

Parking: The car park at the north end of Grasmere Village, near the Village Hall. (GR 337077).

WALK out of the car park and turn right. Cross the bridge over the Rothay then follow the road forking left to emerge on to the A591. Turn left and follow the A591 to the Travellers Rest Pub. Go through the gate opposite the pub, signposted 'Footpath', and follow the wall around the field to 'stepping stones' fording the Tongue Gill. Cross them to a road. Turn left across Low Mill Bridge, spanning Raise Beck, then right. As you walk up the road the rugged cone of Steel Fell rises challengingly ahead. Near the dwellings at Ghyll Foot the road veers right, back over Raise Beck. Leave it and climb straight ahead up the rough drive to the dwelling at 'Helmside'. Go past the house and through a gate. Below you now the Green Burn spills down its slabby gutter, enchanting your ears with Lakeland's signature tune, the sound of cascading water.

Turn right and climb alongside the wall. Steel Fell's south-east ridge is pretty unrelenting. You can, however, follow the advice of the writer Graham Sutton – "A view is like bootlaces; its proper function is to provide excuses for a lot of halts, going up". If you do you'll find that the view over the Vale of Grasmere has been unfolding behind you as you climbed. Eventually, the ridge surrenders and you pant up to the cairn, standing close to a fence, to be greeted, if the mountain gods are smiling upon you, by a 'surprise' view of Thirlmere, the towering spurs of Helvellyn guarding one bank, the easy-angled but boggy and complex folds of Ullscarf the other. In the distance rise Skiddaw and Blencathra.

Descend left alongside the fence. Eventually the wood and wire fence turns away and your path is accompanied only by isolated rusting stanchions of an ancient boundary fence. The path follows a broad grassy ridge curving left, around the head of Greenburn, with the deep trough of Wythburn to your right. Hereabouts, if there's been recent rain, you might stumble into the odd 'spongy bit'. At its lowest point the path passes to the left of a sizeable yet un-named tarn. Now, path and fence begin to climb. Your next objective, Calf Crag, is the obvious rocky summit crowning the skyline ahead, to the left of the fence-posts. At a convenient point leave the fence-posts and climb left on to this summit, whose cairn lies beyond the crest. Far Easedale now curves away below your toe-caps, leading your eye to Wordsworth's 'little Nook of mountain-ground'.

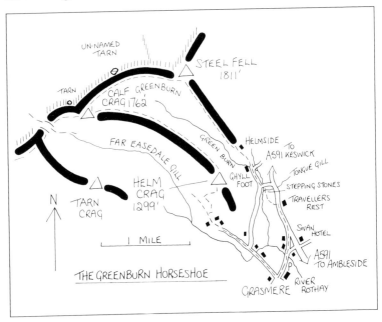

Now follow the well-worn path, left, along the undulating ridge, over Gibson Knott and eventually down to the grassy saddle below Helm Crag. As you go, look across Far Easedale for a glimpse of Easedale Tarn tucked in its shadowy hollow. From the saddle, look left, over Greenburn, at Steel Fell's south-east ridge. You'll swear it looks easier in profile than it felt during the ascent.

Now make the short steep climb onto the rocky crest of Helm Crag. It would appear that in aeons past part of the ridge had collapsed, leaving a crest crowned by rocky pinnacles which lean slightly over a bouldery basin. Exploration of this basin will reveal tiny caves amongst the tumbled boulders. The true summit is not the rocks forming the 'Lion and the Lamb', seen from Grasmere. Rather the pinnacle forming the figures of 'The Old Woman playing an Organ', seen from the A591 as it descends Dunmail Raise. Its ascent requires an awkward scramble, especially if the rock

50

is greasy. Care should be taken, for the summit leans over a considerable drop. This minor fell therefore is one of the rare British summits requiring the use of hands as well as feet to surmount. Given an injection of a thousand foot of Borrowdale Volcanic rock it would become one of Britain's finest peaks!

The first recorded ascent of Helm Crag was made in the late eighteenth-century by a Captain Joseph Budworth, a one-armed veteran of the Siege of Gibraltar. The captain's belt must have been under some strain when he scrambled on to the summit for he and his companions had just demolished a pre-climb snack of – 'stuffed roast port, a boiled fowl, vealed cutlets and ham, beans and bacon, cabbage peas and potatoes, anchovy sauce, parsley and butter, bread and cheese, wheatbread and oatcake, three cups of preserved gooseberries with a bowl of rich cream in the centre' – and all for 10d a head!

Scramble down the 'Lion and the Lamb' rocks on to a grassy ridge where the path veers right. Follow its pleasant serpentines down to join the path in Far Easedale. Turn left to join a tarmac strip which leads across a meadow and into the Easedale Road, which leads down into Grasmere. Turn left to your car.

THIRLMERE

Walk 17

Medium Walk, 6 miles

High Rigg and
St. John's in the Vale

*For many, many years High Rigg would catch my eye as I passed in
bus or car and I would think – 'That looks interesting, I must climb
it sometime'. However I was too busy heading for more glamorous
climbs, peaks, and walks, and decades passed before I set foot on the
fell. Even then High Rigg only served as a 'warm-up' to a 'St. John's
in the Vale Horseshoe' in which the Helvellyn Dodds played the
meatier role. Nevertheless, High Rigg proved to be as 'interesting' as
I had so many fleeting times imagined, worthy in its own right of
inclusion in this book. As well as offering enjoyable walking, by
being somewhat 'off-the-beaten-track' perhaps its main charm is the
exciting but unusual aspects it offers of renowned lakes and fells.
The return walk down a lovely and secluded valley gives a most
pleasant end to the day.*

*Parking: Legburthwaite Car Park and Picnic Site. (GR 318196).
Follow the B5322 where it forks off the A591, Keswick to Ambleside,
near Stanah. Go past the Youth Hostel to reach, on your right, a
pair of semi-detached houses. Turn left into an opening opposite
these houses, by sheds, to reach the car-park.*

GO through the gate at the rear of the car-park on to a road. Turn
left to a gate leading on to the verge of the A591. Turn right over
the bridge spanning St. John's Beck and right again over a stile.
Shortly, the path forks. Take the path climbing left, then left again.
A gruelling climb, twisting through some magnificent pines, now
follows. Only gruelling, however, if you attack it too vigorously or
attempt to surmount it in one go. There's no hurry, stop and turn
and enjoy the view, the crest will come in time.

   Once on the ridge crest, the path descends into a dip before
climbing through a gap in a wall on to a rocky eminence crowned
by a cairn. This is a good spot for a longer 'breather' and chance to
orientate yourself. High Rigg switchbacks ahead, though be assured
you've done all the hard work. Below your toecaps the verdant
carpet of St. John's in the Vale unrolls away seemingly to the
very foot of Blencathra's sharply pleated Threlkeld flank. The
Vale's far boundary rears up dramatically into the gill-cloven flanks
of the Helvellyn Dodds. Look back for a 'peek-a-boo' glimpse
of Thirlmere.

Originally called Leathes Water after the family who owned it, work on converting it into a reservoir began in 1879 and was completed in 1894. Its 58 foot high and 857 foot long masonry dam, one of the first in the country, created a three mile long reservoir containing 9,000,000,000 gallons of water. A 96 mile long tunnel began to supply Mancunians with 36,000,000 gallons of water a day. It is undoubtedly a monument to the skill of Victorian engineers.

Continue along the ridge before swinging left to cross a stile in a fence. Descend slightly left around a hillock, then swing right to a path fork. Follow the left fork along the left side of a hollow. Climb left out of the hollow and down to a stile near a wall corner. Cross this and climb alongside a wall before swinging left then right around a tiny tarn. On a recent May visit I found it carpeted with the lovely pink and white Bogbean, described by William Curtis in his 'Flora Londonensis' as 'one of the most beautiful plants this country can boast'. Continue alongside the wall which shortly veers away. Continue on to the beckoning rocks and cairn that crown the summit of High Rigg.

Though lowly in stature the fell is a splendid viewpoint. Skiddaw is more hard-edged, muscular, than the popular, somewhat matronly, fell seen from Keswick. Blencathra's five ridges – Blease Fell, Gategill, Hallsfell, Doddick, and Scales Fell – are poised like an inverted fan above the roofs of Threlkeld. Below and to the left of Skiddaw, beyond the roofs of Keswick, you should catch a gleam of Derwentwater and Bassenthwaite Lake, whilst beyond them rise the blued and furrowed cones and domes of the Coledale and Newlands fells.

Descend beyond the cairn, twisting left then right into a hollow, then steeply down to emerge on a crossing path near a small plantation. Turn right along this on to tarmac, passing the Carlisle Diocese Youth Centre and a chapel. Just past the chapel you will see a gate/stile on your right, signposted 'Public Bridleway' – St. John's in the Vale'. Ignore this and follow the road a few yards further to see a small gate in the wall below the grassy bank on your right. Go through this gate and down, between becks, to cross a 'clapperbridge' (a stone slab spanning a beck), near their confluence. Continue down to cross a footbridge over a beck then pass between Bridge House and a barn. Turn right past the barn and follow the path along the bank of St. John's Beck.

The rest of your walk is now a delightful stroll back down St. John's in the Vale. Navigation is no problem, the path being amply ornamented with yellow 'footpath' indicators and signs. At points, paths and bridges lead left towards the B5322. Ignore these and keep to the right bank of St. John's Beck throughout. Beyond the fields to your left rise the steep and rugged western flanks of the

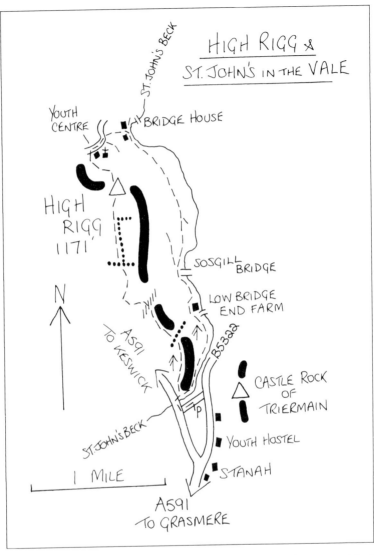

HIGH RIGG & ST. JOHN'S IN THE VALE

ST. JOHN'S BECK

YOUTH CENTRE

BRIDGE HOUSE

HIGH RIGG 1171'

SOSGILL BRIDGE

N

LOW BRIDGE END FARM

A591 TO KESWICK

B5322

CASTLE ROCK OF TRIERMAIN

P

ST. JOHN'S BECK

YOUTH HOSTEL

STANAH

1 MILE

A591 TO GRASMERE

Helvellyn Dodds. They are cloven by gills that offer 'scrambles' for the experienced. Two obviously 'engineered' paths make easier breaches through the crags, one emblazoned with the bizarre name of 'Fisher's Wife's Rake'. This path ends abruptly at a sheepfold called 'Jim's Fold'. Who was Fisher's Wife? Did she have assignations in this lonely spot with the mysterious Jim? Did the cuckolded Fisher hurl her down the 'Rake' to her doom in revenge? The other path, nameless on the map, also ends abruptly at a ruined sheepfold on a high boggy ledge.

Pause on the beck bank just beyond Sosgill Bridge and look back. The beck, the gracefully arched bridge, and the spiny ridges of Blencathra rising beyond are worth a shot or two if you are a photographer. Just before Low Bridge End Farm 'footpath' signs direct you above and behind the farm before returning to the beck side. Ahead, dominating the narrowing mouth of the Vale, is Castle Rock of Triermain. Some of the hardest rock-climbs in Lakeland trace their vertiginous way up its oftimes overhanging crags. Sir Walter Scott (or was it Tennyson?), wrote an epic poem in which Castle Rock featured as a stronghold of the legendary King Arthur. The fellside on your right now begins to squeeze in and the path is forced into a final climb across a wooded fellside dropping steeply into the beck, before swinging right then down to the stile leading onto the A591.

ULLSWATER

The Helvellyn Edges

Striding Edge is undoubtedly the most popular way up Helvellyn from the east. It is the lure that attracts walkers of all ages and all standards to this side of the mountain. It would be impossible to leave it out of any walking guidebook to the Ullswater area. A traverse of Striding Edge takes a step beyond simple fellwalking. Given dry, calm conditions, however, the reader of this booklet who has done the Rough Crag-Long Stile ridge and the St. Sunday Crag-Cofa Pike ridge should have no problem. The round of Striding Edge and Swirrel Edge gives one of the most exciting day's fell-walking that Lakeland can offer.

Parking: The car-park in Glenridding (GR 386169).

GO back to the main road, turn right over the bridge, and right again up the lane past the climbing shop. Continue until the path forks. Take the right-hand fork, signposted 'Greenside', to go between the beck and the campsite to reach and cross a stone bridge. Beyond this turn left up a rough track alongside a wall to a gate/stile signposted 'Helvellyn via Mires Beck'. Cross this and climb left to a similar sign on a wall directing you right up to a gate/stile in a wall corner. Beyond this turn left across a footbridge over a beck. Now climb the path up the right bank of Mires Beck, shortly crossing over to the left bank. A long steepish climb follows, the path eventually climbing alongside a wall, before the grassy summit of Birkhouse Moor, 2355 feet, is attained. The view back of the constant changes of light on the shining reaches of Ullswater is a good excuse for 'breathers'. Some 'peak-baggers' lists credit Birkhouse Moor with three summits but I feel that's a trifle generous. My list makes the highest point just to the right of the wall corner where the wall veers south-westerly towards Striding Edge. The 2½" map argues for the next bump that way – take your pick!

Hopefully, displayed before you now are the famous 'edges', enfolding the high corrie cupping Red Tarn and airily linking Helvellyn's 'table mountain' with conical Catstycam. Perhaps I should liken Helvellyn more to a giant aircraft carrier. In 1926 two daring young men landed their flying machine upon its summit then, more daringly, took off from it. A memorial to this feat stands just south of the summit shelter.

Continue, a little swampily, alongside the wall until it turns away at the Hole-in-the-Wall and you start the climb towards Striding

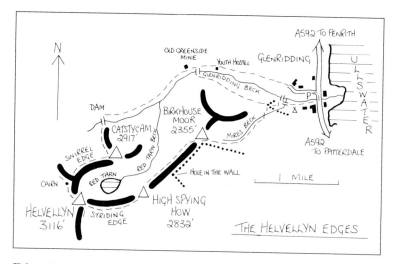

The Helvellyn Edges

Edge. Leave the worn path and climb the obvious summit overlooking the start of the 'edge' proper. This is High Spying How, 2832 feet, and listed as a separate peak.

Once on Striding Edge the way is obvious. Don't be deterred by the metal cross just below and to the left after the first narrow section, a memorial to an unfortunate follower of foxhounds, the danger is more apparent than real. Unless you find it too scary, or ice and snow conditions forcibly prevent it, attempt to keep to the crest all the way. This gives the excitement, fun and satisfaction that is the point of an ascent by this route. The most difficult section is the climb down into the gap at the end of the Edge, but even here the holds are large and firm. Beyond this gap there is another hump of rock to scramble over and then the route degenerates into a steep, shaly pant up onto the fell rim, emerging near a memorial to a doggy who maintained a long and loyal vigil over the corpse of his master, earning poetic praise from Wordsworth and Sir Walter Scott. There is a school of thought, admittedly largely composed of cat lovers, who believe faithful Fido fortified himself with a bit of Master!

Walk right along the rim of the fell shortly to reach the invariably crowded wind shelter just below the summit. Climb up onto the summit rocks of Helvellyn, 3116 feet. The view from Helvellyn is panoramic and I have not the space to describe it. It is a good place, on a clear windless day, to take your map out and orientate yourself to the splendours of Lakeland spread at your feet.

Walk north-westerly along the rim, passing the slightly lower trig-point, to a cairn on the rim, where it veers west-north-westerly, marking the start of the descent onto Swirrel Edge. After heavy snowfalls, large cornices build up along this rim. In 'white-out' conditions they can, and have been, death traps for the unwary. Swirrel Edge is much easier and shorter than its big brother across Red Tarn, only a couple of rocky steps requiring care. At its lowest point a path forks right, down towards Red Tarn. Ignore this and climb along the ridge, broad and easy now, onto the narrow summit of Catstycam, 2917 feet, a graceful, relatively unfrequented peak, a splendid viewpoint, and worth every gasp of extra effort.

Turn left and descend a steepish stony path down the fell's north west ridge to a 'busted' dam spanning the Glenridding Beck. In the 1920's water was stored in Keppel Cove, to your left, to power the Greenside Lead Mine smelters. The dam burst, loosing millions of gallons of water which, clawing up boulders and trees en route, poured into Glenridding village causing extensive damage but fortunately no loss of life. Cross the crest of the dam. If it's at all gusty you will probably regard this crossing as more scary than anything on the famous 'edges'. I know I have.

Follow the track on the far side down to the buildings of the old Greenside Lead Mine, now an outdoor pursuits centre. The mine was in production from 1780 to 1962, producing over one quarter of a million tons of lead concentrate. Just above the buildings cross back over the Glenridding Beck by a footbridge and turn left along a pleasant path traversing below the steep craggy Blea Cove flank of Birkhouse Moor to rejoin your outward route at a gate/stile.

Warning: When plastered with snow and ice this walk is a different proposition. It should not be attempted without the proper equipment, ice axe, crampons, and possibly a rope, and the ability to use them.

St. Sunday Crag and Fairfield

A splendid high-level walk giving superb and constantly changing views, and a flavour of mountaineering in the crossing of Cofa Pike, undoubtedly the finest of the ridges radiating from Fairfield. In hard winter conditions, however, this route should not be attempted without an ice-axe, and the ability to use it. A 'white-out', snow combined with mist, turns the Fairfield summit plateau into a hazardous place. In such conditions careful attention must be paid to navigation.

Parking: There is a 'Pay/Stay' car-park opposite the Patterdale Hotel, and limited parking in the mouth of the lane leading into Grisedale. (GR 391162).

WALK up the winding lane to Grisedale for about half a mile. After passing a white house, on your right, a gate will be seen on your left signposted 'Public Footpath'. Go through this and shortly beyond bear right, either through a metal gate or over a stile, and follow the path climbing steeply up the fellside. This passes through trees before emerging onto the open fell once more. Behind, there is a fine view down onto the head of Ullswater. Beyond the far ridge of Grisedale, its flank scarred by the worn 'trod' slanting up towards Striding Edge, rise high shapely Catstycam and bluff lowly Sheffield Pike.

Continue to a stile over a wall. Beyond this the path flanks across a steep fellside for about three hundred yards before dividing, near a cairn. The lower, right-hand path circumvents the outlying summit of Birks. Unless time is short I see no merit in this for Birks is the natural beginning to this fine ridge. Climb steeply up to the left, the path bearing further left as the angle eases, before curving back rightwards towards the small cairn that crowns the broad grassy summit. The dominating feature of the view is the challenging profile of St. Sunday Crag, your next objective. Dove Crag and Hart Crag, Fairfield outliers, peer around its left hand profile and Helvellyn has now expanded in more detail to its right.

Head easily down to the saddle below St. Sunday Crag and a junction with the flanking path previously mentioned. The summit is reached by climbing directly up the ridge ahead or by a path, which appears to have lost favour over the years, slanting leftwards across the face of the fell. The cairn stands near the southern rim of the stony summit dome. Helvellyn, Striding Edge and the splendid coves and ridges of Dollywaggon and Nethermost Pikes

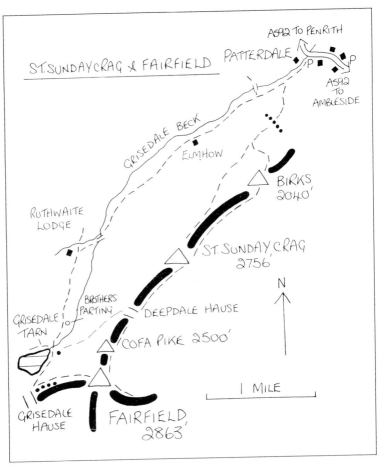

ST. SUNDAY CRAG & FAIRFIELD

A592 TO PENRITH
PATTERDALE
A592 TO AMBLESIDE

GRISEDALE BECK

ELMHOW

BIRKS 2040'

RUTHWAITE LODGE

ST. SUNDAY CRAG 2756'

N

BROTHERS PARTING

DEEPDALE HAUSE

GRISEDALE TARN

COFA PIKE 2500'

1 MILE

GRISEDALE HAUSE

FAIRFIELD 2863'

are seen to advantage from here. Dominating the scene, however, is the rugged, massive north-east face of Fairfield, particularly if draped in snow. Cofa Pike, your next target, virtually disappears into the stark backcloth of its giant neighbour.

Go south-westerly along a ridge which steepens and narrows as it drops down to Deepdale Hause. It has been my frequent experience to meet a strong wind on this section of the ridge. Presumably the prevailing westerlies, frustrated by the mountain wall of Helvellyn and Fairfield, scream into the gap filled by Grisedale Tarn, ahead and below, and are funnelled directly at Deepdale Hause. On the hause a cairn marks the beginning of a path which slants down to reach Grisedale Tarn near its exit beck. This is a useful escape route if required.

Steep rocky climbing follows to reach the narrow and enjoyable summit ridge of Cofa Pike. Beyond, a short dip is followed by a stiffish scree slope to reach the broad summit plateau of Fairfield. The view is extensive. Highlights are the gleaming waters of Windermere, Esthwaite and Coniston to the south; beyond glints Morecambe Bay. Westerly the thrusting dome of Gable dominates a superb mountain skyline ranging from Coniston Old Man to Grisedale Pike. Helvellyn and its splendid outliers sprawl across the northern sky. From the north-eastern rim there is an interesting bird's-eye view into rugged Sleet Cove, dominated by Hutaple Crag. This rim is where the danger lies in a 'white-out', for large cornices build up here.

Two stone 'shelters' crown Fairfield, one balanced on the north-eastern rim, the other further west and more central. North of this second shelter a cairn stands on a rocky plinth. From this latter cairn a line of cairns heads west, across the plateau. Follow these. They lead to a steep and eroded path which eventually runs down alongside an old wall and into the narrow saddle of Grisedale Hause. The fell rising steeply beyond is Seat Sandal.

Turn right here and follow the path past the dark waters of Grisedale Tarn. Legend has it that the huge cairn on Dunmail Raise marks the site of the battle where Dunmail, the last native king of Cumberland, was defeated by the Anglo-Saxons. Survivors from the slaughter are reputed to have fled up to Grisedale Tarn where they flung Dunmail's crown into the water. Their ghosts are purported to repeat this act. Fact or fiction, the truth lies some-where between, for history tells us that King Dunmail died in Rome, with his boots on.

Cross Grisedale Beck, where it issues from the tarn, by stepping stones. Notice the escape route from Deepdale Hause coming down to your right. Beyond the beck the path swings right and down, under the steep buttresses of Tarn and Falcon Crags. Shortly after beginning the descent from the tarn look across to your right to spot a T-shaped metal memorial crowning an outcrop of rock. This is known as The Brothers' Parting. Here Wordsworth is said to have bid farewell to his younger and sailor brother John who was subsequently drowned in a shipwreck.

The path continues down to pass Ruthwaite Lodge, now the weekend home of the Sheffield University Mountaineering Club. This now well-maintained structure was a chilly shell, deep in sheep droppings, when I first sought shelter in it on a wild winter's day in 1951. Behind the hut lovely cascades spill out of the lonely recesses of Ruthwaite Cove. Below the hut the path divides. Take the right fork which leads down to a footbridge over the Grisedale Beck. The path now leads you pleasantly back down the valley and eventually to your car. Glance back occasionally at the splendid mix of sharp ridges and rugged hanging valleys.

Place Fell and the Ullswater Shore Path

A fairly long but entertaining walk which is nowhere strenuous, all the hard work being done in the first three miles. The view from Place Fell is superb and on the flanks of this isolated fell there is always the chance of spotting red deer. The shore path is delightful, possibly the best of its kind in Lakeland, offering more fine, and constantly changing, views and the opportunity of a swim or a lakeside picnic.

Parking: In the Pay/Stay car-park opposite the Patterdale Hotel. (GR 396158).

WALK south through Patterdale village, passing the White Lion Hotel, to where a bridge on your left spans Goldrill Beck. Cross the bridge and follow the road into the hamlet of Rooking where it curves left to a gate leading to the open fellside. Go through the gate, cross a footbridge over a beck and climb the path slanting steeply right up the fellside, ultimately to emerge on to the grassy saddle of Boardale Hause. Surprisingly, I've spotted deer on the fellside below this popular path. Look for a metal manhole cover in the rear left-hand corner of this flattish saddle. Follow a path past this which shortly turns left to pass a small sheepfold and begins to climb towards the steep summit slopes of Place Fell. Steeper zig-zags eventually take you on to the left-hand skyline where a shaly gully leads up to the cairn crowning the subsidiary summit of Round How and the end of all the 'hard graft'. Easy walking along the westerly rim of the fell leads to the rocky tor and trig-point crowning Place Fell, 2,155 feet.

This summit is an ideal vantage point for taking out your map and orientating yourself with the Helvellyn/Fairfield fells, given of course that you can see them or there's not a map-snatching wind gusting across the summit. Their rugged ice-honed eastern flanks are particularly detailed. Away to the north-west Blencathra displays its fluted Threlkeld flank, with a retiring flat-topped Skiddaw to its left. Northwards, through the gap between Carrock Fell and isolated Great Mell Fell, lie the Solway Firth and Scotland.

To descend, follow a well-worn path north-easterly, passing to the left of a small tarn, down to an obvious sheepfold on the grassy saddle of Low Moss.

Pass to the right of the sheepfold and when the path forks turn left and follow the path down the right bank of Low Moss Gill.

The path improves as you descend and eventually passes a derelict quarry building. Below this building the path splits. Keep to the left-hand fork. Across to your left Scalehow Beck tumbles out of a hanging valley to merge with Low Moss Gill. Your path heads down towards the fine cascades below this junction. Ahead the view down the lower reaches of Ullswater widens impressively with every turn of the path. The path touches the edges of the beck then swings away to the right where it passes between some large boulders. Hereabouts it splits, with a fork heading down steep grass to meet a lower path. Go down this fork. Turn left along the lower path to cross Scalehow Beck by a footbridge. Beyond the bridge the path climbs up towards a gate then swings left just before reaching it to climb steeply up alongside a wall. Follow the path around the wall corner and when it divides take the upper fork. The prominent fell across the lake is Gowbarrow Fell; along the lakeshore at its foot Wordsworth saw his famed daffodils. The castle-like structure is Lyulph's Tower.

As the path picks its delightful way across the steep, rocky, lake-lapped base of Place Fell the view ahead constantly varies. At first the eye looks deep into Glencoynedale, guarded by Greenside and the dark rocky bulk of Sheffield Pike. As you go, Birkhouse Moor, Catstycam and the eastern ridges of Nethermost Pike and Dolly-waggon Pike slowly march into view. Roughly a mile and a half after rounding the wall corner Silver Bay and its pebbly beach is reached. Here the path divides near a large cairn. Take the left-hand path, up a rocky ravine, to reach a grassy saddle and fine viewpoint. Distantly ahead is the gap of Kirkstone Pass, dividing John Bell's Banner, on the left, from Red Screes. Below, in the foreground, is Patterdale village. Further right, across the head of Ullswater, you look into Grisedale, with distant Seat Sandal at its head. To its left St. Sunday Crag bulks large, whilst to its right are arrayed the fine eastern coves and ridges of Dollywaggon Pike, Nethermost Pike and Striding Edge. Your way lies ahead along the path traversing the fellside. It is well-constructed and as you go you will realise why, passing below, above and through derelict slate quarries.

When this path forks continue with the left-hand path slanting across the fellside. It passes an iron seat, dips down, near an old quarry, then divides, with a branch curving down to the right. Ignore this right-hand fork and continue leftwards, crossing the site of another old quarry before dropping down to the footbridge you crossed on your outward journey. Go through the gate and the hamlet of Rooking back to your car.

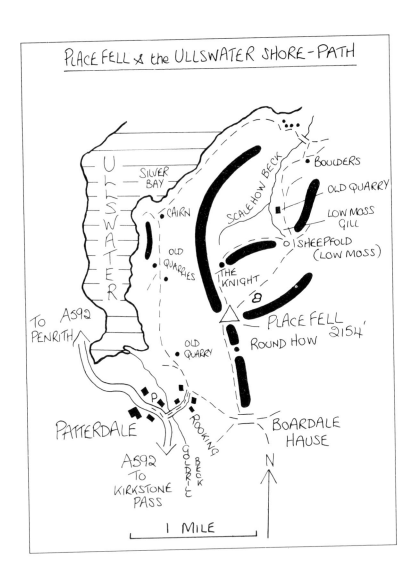

PLACE FELL & the ULLSWATER SHORE-PATH

Hallin Fell

An easy walk combining a superb viewpoint with a delightful lakeshore stroll. Can be done independently or combined with Walk 22, Pikeawassa and Martindale, to make a longer and even more varied expedition.

Parking: From Pooley Bridge take the road signposted 'Howtown', along the south-eastern shore of Ullswater. Park in the old quarry on the right of the road just beyond the crest of the fierce Howtown zig-zags, and opposite St. Peter's church. (GR 435193).

FOLLOW the worn grassy path starting from the left-hand end of the quarry. A short distance above the start you pass, on your left, a wall corner, where a drystone wall veers away across the flank of the fell. Store this detail in your memory before climbing on.

Hallin Fell is crowned by a beautifully constructed cairn. The all-round view is superb, although somewhat restricted to the south and east by the neighbouring fells. Below you Ullswater stretches out its shining levels to either hand. Stand facing the lake and the neighbouring fell to your left is Place Fell. To the right of this, but distantly, can be seen a flat-topped Helvellyn framed between Striding Edge, on the left, and the delectably sculpted Catstycam. Below and to the right of Catstycam the dark bulk of Sheffield Pike overlooks Glenridding. The rounded Helvellyn Dods march away from Sheffield Pike towards distant Skiddaw. East of Skiddaw rises gracefully fluted Blencathra followed by its more mundane neighbours Bannerdale Crags and Bowscale Fell. In the foreground Gowbarrow Fell looms over the lake, with the tree-dotted dome of Great Mell Fell to its right. Away to your right the hamlet of Pooley Bridge nestles at the foot of Ullswater with the distant Pennines rising beyond. Blocking the eastern view is neighbouring, beacon-topped, Bonscale Pike, a northern 'tail-ender' of the long High Street range. This range marches away southwards in a succession of bulky fells the farthest of which, Rampsgill Head, commanding the head of Martindale, hides High Street. In the foreground perky Pikeawassa splits the lower reaches of Martindale from narrow Fusedale, tucked in the shadow of Loadpot Hill. Lower Martindale is dominated by The Nab, above and beyond which Rest Dod, an insignificant fell from most view-points, shows a fine profile. The craggy ridge of Beda Fell divides Martindale from Boardale. This ridge is topped by the startlingly spiky summit, seen from this viewpoint, of the highest Angle Tarn

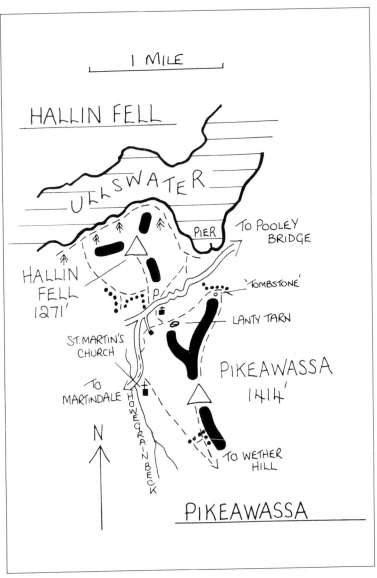

1 MILE

HALLIN FELL

ULLSWATER

PIER

TO POOLEY BRIDGE

HALLIN FELL 1271'

'TOMBSTONE'

P

LANTY TARN

ST. MARTIN'S CHURCH

TO MARTINDALE

PIKEAWASSA 1414'

N

HOWEGRAIN BECK

TO WETHER HILL

PIKEAWASSA

Pike. Bulky Place Fell forms Boardale's western wall and we have come the full scenic circle.

After digesting this splendid feast of visual delights return down to the previously mentioned wall corner. Turn right here and make your way along faint paths through the bracken, alongside the wall. After about four hundred yards the wall turns downhill, whilst ahead a further wall comes up to take its place. In the gap between these walls a better path, slanting up from the left, will be met. Follow this path, to go alongside a wall and eventually down into trees and a junction with a lakeshore path just to the right of a gate. Turn right and follow the shore path, always keeping to the left when any apparent diversion appears. Beyond an obvious rocky headland, Kailpot Crag, the path emerges from the trees and begins to slant rightwards and uphill, eventually with a wall on its left. Ignore a gate in this wall, with an obvious footpath beyond, and continue following the wall. Shortly the path divides. Take the broad grassy right-hand path which climbs steadily uphill, aloof to the squealing tyres and the grinding gears on the nearby zig-zags, to return you to your car.

An interesting climax to the day is to stroll across the road and visit the beautifully maintained little upland church of St. Peter's of Martindale.

Pikeawassa and Martindale

Less frequented than neighbouring Hallin Fell, Walk 21, with which it could be combined. Demands a little more 'puff' but worth the effort for the view from its pleasant summit ridge and spiky top. For those interested in such things the old church of St. Martin, with its once-pagan font and eight hundred years old yew tree, only adds more pleasure to an enjoyable short walk.

Parking: As for Walk 21.

WALK to the right of the church, and alongside a wall, to reach tiny Lanty Tarn. Turn left here and follow a good grassy path which slants gently down across the fellside. Eventually a wall climbs up from the left to run alongside the path. Now keep your eyes open for a small metal manhole cover in the path with a tombstone-like stone marker on the right of the path, just before a rocky outcrop on your right.

Climb the bank above the 'tombstone' onto a sloping grassy shelf. Look for a narrow path climbing slightly right. Follow this path which climbs steeply to the right of the rocks above. Eventually the angle eases, the odd cairn appears, and the path improves to follow the crest of a pleasant, rock-encrusted ridge. Pause for a breather and a fine view back down the lower reaches of Ullswater.

Continue your climb, with the angle easing, the ridge broadening and the view expanding with every upward step. To the right, across the deep furrows of Martindale and Boardale, looms Place Fell. A keen eye might spot the topmost spire of Catstycam peeking over its rim. Left of Place Fell, St. Sunday Crag dramatically fills the gap in the skyline left by Boardale Hause. Tucked in behind St. Sunday Crag is higher Fairfield, with Cofa Pike perched like a parrot on its shoulder. Ahead, beyond the fell crest, The Nab spires out of the depths of Martindale, with Rest Dod looming above and beyond. Far Rampsgill Head, the northern bastion of High Street and 'King of the Martindale Fells', blocks the head of the valley. To your left, across the depths of the lonely valley of Fusedale, rise the brawny gill-furrowed flanks of Loadpot Hill and Wether Hill.

Continue beyond the last cairn to reach the spiky rocks that form the summit of Pikeawassa. Follow the path beyond the summit and down to pass through a gap in a wall. Then turn right and descend steeply alongside the wall to shortly reach a lower, well-used, path.

Pause here and look left down into Martindale where a red-roofed building will be spotted rising above the trees. This is The Bungalow, formerly a shooting-lodge of the Earls of Lonsdale, where the Kaiser, Wilhelm II, stayed as a guest prior to the First World War. Ironically, during the Second World War, it sheltered the somewhat spartan Officer's Mess of a battle camp established in the valley. The sparse trees clinging to the fellside below your feet are reputedly one of the remaining areas of relict or native woodland left in Lakeland.

Now turn right, back through the wall, and follow the path pleasantly down to the rear of the old church of St. Martin. A visit to this plain, sturdy upland chapel, with its quiet atmosphere of devotion and history, is a highlight of this walk.

Leaving the church, follow the road towards Howtown. About four hundred yards on look for a gate, signposted 'Footpath to Howtown' on the wall to its right. Go through the gate and follow the path beyond to the dwelling at 'Cotehow'. Pass to the front of the house, across its drive, and climb a grassy path around to a gate and shortly beyond to reach Lanty Tarn. The church of St. Peter, near the car park, is also worth a visit, though it lacks the atmosphere of times past.

BROTHERSWATER

John Bell's Banner.

John Bell's Banner looks like a 'pudden' of a fell from most angles but it is one for the connoisseur, continually revealing interesting facets for those who trouble to look. An enjoyable and varied short walk with all the hard work over in the first mile.

Parking: In the lay-by just north of the bridge over the Caudale Beck, about quarter of a mile south of the Brotherswater Hotel, on the A592. (GR 403115).

GO through the metal gate on the south side of the bridge and follow the path above and parallel to the beck. After a while it spirals right onto a steep, well-defined grassy ridge. This zig-zagging hollowed path is the remains of an old 'sledgate' and eventually it slants away along the left flank of the ridge to reach ruined quarry buildings overlooking the lonely hanging valley of Caudale. Men used to steer sleds, or trailbarrows, loaded with a quarter of a ton of slate down this path, running before them like a horse, then hauling the empty sled back uphill and repeating the performance. One Honister quarryman, Joseph Clarke of Stonethwaite, is recorded as having shifted five tons of slate and covered seventeen miles in seventeen successive journeys.

If you slant left and explore the ruins be careful as there is at least one crudely covered and evil-looking hole. The high mountain sanctuary of Caudale is a favourite feeding place for red deer. Climb back up on to the crest of the ridge to regain the path. Behind and below you lies Brotherswater, with a glimpse of Ullswater beyond. Across the A592 you look into the depths of Dovedale, dominated by the pale steep walls of Dove Crag, with the eastern skyline of Fairfield and St. Sunday Crag rising beyond.

Continue up the ridge which gradually levels out onto the summit plateau where a large cairn, marked 2,474 feet on both large and small O.S. maps, is reached. Head south-easterly, passing to the right of a small tarn, to meet the wall and the path climbing up from Kirkstone Pass. Turn left and follow this to reach the junction of walls that crowns the broad summit of this fell. Go through a gap in the crossing wall to reach the cairn. To the north-west there is a distant but comprehensive view of the rugged eastern flanks of Fairfield and Helvellyn. To the east, across Threshthwaite Mouth, the graceful summit cairn of Thornthwaite Crag beckons, with the

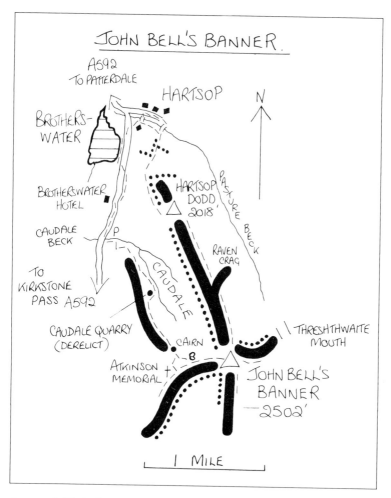

dome of High Street to its left. Froswick and Ill Bell look their shapely best to the south-east and below them the green hollow of Troutbeck leads the eye down to gleaming Windermere.

This sprawling fell has two other names, Caudale Moor and Stony Cove Pike, but I prefer the bold ringing sound of John Bell's Banner. About 350 years ago the curate of Ambleside was one John Bell and his parish boundary ran across the summit of this fell. The local name for boundary being 'banner' this mountain signified, in the eyes of his flock, the limit of both his spiritual and temporal ministrations.

To continue, return to the gap in the wall but do not go through it. Instead, turn right and walk alongside the wall, to shortly meet and climb over a joining wall. Continue alongside the original wall, following it down a broad grassy ridge into a dip below Hartsop Dodd. Over the wall, beyond the bowl of Caudale, you will see the ruined workshops of Caudale Quarry tucked in the flank of your ridge of ascent. Follow the wall up on to the summit of Hartsop Dodd. Go through a gap to the cairn then continue with the wall now on your right. When the wall turns away follow cairns down an ever-steepening path giving a 'birds-eye' view of Hartsop, the Vale of Patterdale, and the head of Ullswater. Glance left into Dovedale, where the sinking sun may be highlighting the ancient 'standing stones' in the fields at the valley mouth. When you meet a wall corner turn right and follow the wall down to a gate. Continue steeply, and soggily hereabouts, trying not to splatter on to your 'bum', down to a bridge spanning the Pasture Beck. Cross it and walk through the car park into the hamlet of Hartsop.

With its spinning-galleries, old corn-drying kiln, allied to the neighbouring ruins of a lead mine and the old quarry workings in Caudale, Hartsop retains aspects of a time when many of Lakeland's loveliest corners were self-sufficient units of rural industry. As you follow the road through the hamlet look for a gap between buildings on your left leading down to a footbridge back over the Pasture Beck. Cross this and follow the delightful lane beyond which eventually brings you out onto the A592. Cross the road and go through a kissing-gate signposted 'National Trust, Brotherswater'. Beyond this bear left and follow a path along the wooded eastern shore of the lake which eventually climbs back up onto the road. Turn right along the road for a short distance keeping your eyes open for a kissing-gate signposted 'National Trust' opposite. Go through this and turn right to follow a path running above and parallel to the road.

When opposite the Brotherswater Hotel gates lead back onto the road. You could take advantage of these to down a refreshing pint before walking the few hundred yards back up the road to your car.

HAWESWATER

Small Water, Harter Fell
and Gatesgarth Pass

This must be one of the most enjoyable short mountain walks in Lakeland. The ascent passes through some rugged scenery which is enhanced by a splendid mountain tarn. The descent goes over more amiable ground giving a bird's-eye view of Haweswater.

Parking: In the car-park at the Haweswater road-end. (GR 469108).

LEAVE the car-park shortly to reach a three-fingered signpost near a wall corner. Follow the path directly ahead signposted 'Public Bridleway to Kentmere'. This well-worn path slants gradually upwards under the green and grotty crags and gullies on the north-eastern flank of Harter Fell. It steepens for the final climb to Small Water, crossing a tributary of Small Water Beck by a clapper bridge and then the beck proper by stepping stones where it empties from the tarn.

Small Water, framed between a rugged flank of Harter Fell and the crags of Mardale Ill Bell, which look steep enough to tempt the passing rock-climber, is a gem of a mountain tarn. Here rock and water, the quintessence of Lakeland fell scenery, are sublimely matched. Above and beyond the tarn hangs the rocky notch of Nan Bield Pass, your next objective.

To reach this follow the path around to the right of the tarn and pass across the scree and boulders lying below the crags. The stone structures hereabouts were, according to Mr. Wainwright, shelters built for the protection of travellers, long before the days of frivolous fellwalkers, overtaken by bad weather when crossing Nan Bield. A final steep climb leads up and into its narrow portals, crowned by a well-constructed windbreak. Beyond and below Kentmere Reservoir nestles in the shadow of a volcano-like Ill Bell. Leftwards, or south-easterly, from Nan Bield a nicely stepped ridge, with just enough rock bursting through to give it a mountain flavour, leads pleasantly to the broad grassy summit of Harter Fell.

The summit cairn incorporates remnants of the old iron boundary fence, giving the appearance of a stand of surrealist weaponry, especially when fronded with ice. The best of the view, for me, is the detailed prospect of the rugged eastern flank of High Street. Deep Blea Water peeps dourly around a flank of Mardale Ill Bell

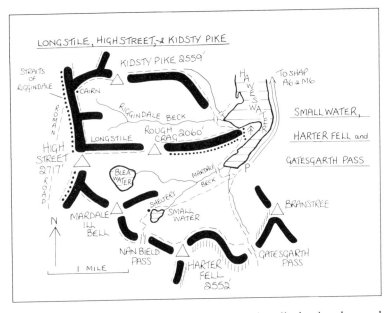

LONGSTILE, HIGHSTREET, & KIDSTY PIKE

KIDSTY PIKE 2559'

STRAITS OF RIGGINDALE

CAIRN

RIGGINDALE BECK

ROMAN ROAD

LONGSTILE

ROUGH CRAG 2060'

HIGH STREET 2717'

ROAD

BLEA WATER

MARDALE BECK

SHELTERS

SMALL WATER

HAWESWATER

TO SHAP A6 & M6

SMALL WATER,

HARTER FELL and

GATESGARTH PASS

P

BRANSTREE

N

MARDALE ILL BELL

NAN BIELD PASS

HARTER FELL 2552'

GATESGARTH PASS

1 MILE

and shapely Kidsty Pike, balanced on its rocky plinth, rises beyond the serrated Long Stile/Rough Crag ridge. Far away to the south-east the hump of Yorkshire's Ingleborough may be picked out. Far to the west, Gable's tilted 'bowler' is easily picked out, with a 'sliced off' Pillar to its right and a jumble of Scafells, Bowfell, and Crinkles to its left.

Just beyond the cairn a wood and wire fence marches across the summit, providing a useful aid to navigation, given bad conditions, all the way down to Gatesgarth Pass. Follow this fence leftwards, north-easterly, and down to a lower, iron-armoured cairn. Beyond this the ground steepens a little before the fence veers abruptly right. Walk to the rocks on the edge here for a superb aerial view of Haweswater Reservoir – a view marred, in my opinion, by the exposed and unnatural beach contour and the added pathos of the lanes and intake walls emerging from the drowned valley. In the boiling summer of '84 the rapidly retreating water revealed the ruins of the drowned village of Mardale Green and brought traffic-jams and ice-cream vendors to this normally tranquil valley.

Bear right and follow the fence down until just above the grassy saddle of Gatesgarth Pass where the path veers away and down to cut a corner. Turn left from the gate crowning the pass and follow the good path back down to the car-park.

Long Stile, High Street and Kidsty Pike

A friend of mine, whose knowledge of Lakeland is encyclopaedic, claims that the Rough Crag-Long Stile ridge is the finest ridge in Lakeland. I cannot bring myself entirely to agree with him but will go as far as to say that it is the most entertaining way to climb High Street. It is nowhere as slender or airy as the more glamorous 'edges', like Sharp, Striding or Swirrel, but it is longer, and for the peak-bagger has the added bonus of two-thousand footer Rough Crag.

Parking: As for Walk 24.

GO beyond the car-park shortly to reach a three-fingered signpost near a wall corner. Turn right and follow the sign 'Public Footpath To Bampton'. This goes down, alongside a wall and crossing several boggy patches by duckboards, to a footbridge over the Mardale Beck. Beyond the bridge turn right and follow the path leading out onto the wooded spur, The Rigg, that divides the headwaters of the reservoir. This path presently slants up to the left towards the crest of the spur, to a gap in a wall, to the left of the trees. Before reaching the gap a path bears left through the bracken. Follow this to meet the wall crowning the crest of the ridge. Turn left, along it. It is impossible to go astray because the ridge is well-defined, the Riggindale flank falling away precipitously. The wall turns down into Riggindale just below the summit of Rough Crag.

Beyond Rough Crag the ridge drops down to the grassy saddle, and tarn, of Caspel Gate before rearing up again in the slender ridge that is Long Stile proper. Below, to your left, Blea Water, 'the black water', invariably lives up to its name. In the fifties a Brathay Hall exploration group were stunned to record a plummetting depth of over two-hundred feet for this sombre tarn. Long Stile offers no problem in normal conditions but when plastered with snow or ice can become a serious proposition and should not be attempted unless the proper equipment is carried. When the rim of the fell is reached walk south-west across the grass to reach the trig point, and the wall that marches across the fell's broad and grassy dome.

High Street takes its name from the Roman military road that once ran across it, connecting the forts sited near Ambleside and Penrith. Cartographers in the thirteenth century referred to it as 'Brettestreete', or the 'street of the Britons', which suggests this is one of the ancient highways of England. One can see the advantages

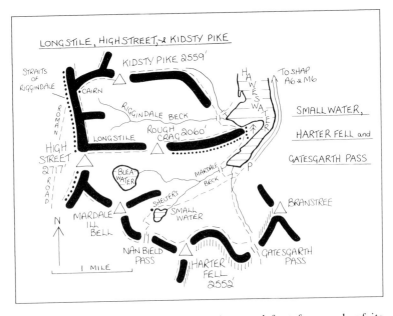

LONGSTILE, HIGHSTREET, & KIDSTY PIKE

KIDSTY PIKE 2559'

STRAITS
OF
RIGGINDALE

CAIRN

ROMAN

RIGGINDALE BECK

ROUGH
CRAG 2060'

LONGSTILE

HIGH
STREET
2717'

ROAD

BLEA
WATER

MARDALE
BECK

SHELTERS

N

MARDALE
ILL
BELL

SMALL
WATER

NAN BIELD
PASS

HARTER
FELL
2552'

BRANSTREE

GATESGARTH
PASS

1 MILE

HAWESWATER

TO SHAP
A6 & M6

SMALL WATER,

HARTER FELL and

GATESGARTH PASS

to our forebears. Well above two thousand feet for much of its length it would be clear of even the highest forest which would mean faster travel and freedom from possible ambush. The Romans would be quick to grasp these advantages, although the thoughts of a raw 'sprog' from the Mediterranean coast sloshing his way across the unprotected summit dome in the teeth of a wet Lakeland spring gale must have been unprintable. The line of the military road shows up best when the mountain is covered in snow. Both from north and south it can be clearly seen climbing across the western shoulders of the summit dome, and late afternoon or evening light highlights its zig-zag descent down the western flank of Froswick into the head of Troutbeck. On the large O.S. map High Street is also christened Racecourse Hill, a relic from the days, prior to 1885, when it was the site of annual shepherds' meets, when strays were handed back to their owners. This was as much a social as a business gathering and horse racing, wrestling and other appropriate Cumbrian junketings went on. The prospect from High Street is wide-ranging but distant, everything close at hand being hidden by the spread of the summit dome. It is from the rims, looking down on Blea Water or Hayes Water, that the most dramatic views are seen.

For the descent head north along the wall eventually to drop down to the saddle of the Straits of Riggindale. Continue with the wall steeply up the far side until a path branching off to the right, marked with a cairn, is reached. Follow this – it leads around the rim of Riggindale to a cluster of rocks. At this point the Roman Road bears away north-easterly. You continue with the path along the rim, with the drop to your right. This path drops down to a broad grassy saddle before rising up to the airy summit of Kidsty Pike. High Street looks impressive, across the gulf of Riggindale, the 'Roman Road' slung over its western shoulder. Through the Straits of Riggindale there's a distant glimpse of the Coniston fells.

Riggindale is the haunt of Lakeland's Golden Eagles and if you keep your eyes open you may be lucky enough to spot one of these magnificent birds.

A path leads easily down the eastern ridge, climbs over the rocky hiccup of Kidsty Howes, then threads steeply down between rocky outcrops, followed by steep grass, to reach a footbridge over the Riggindale Beck. Cross the bridge and follow the path, often passing between stone uprights, around the lakeshore and up to the crest of The Rigg to meet your outward route.

KESWICK

Skiddaw via Longside Edge

Almost invariably the 'tourist' routes to the tops of the major Lakeland fells are the most uninteresting. The Jenkin Path up Skiddaw is no exception to this rule, being a long boring trudge. Offered below is a more varied and entertaining way to Skiddaw's hoary and boot-battered dome.

Parking: In the Forestry Association Dodd Wood/Mirehouse Sawmill car-park on the A591 Keswick-Carlisle road, just over four miles north-west of Keswick (GR 235282).

RETURN to the A591 and turn right. Follow its right-hand verge for just under a mile to reach a narrow, fenced path climbing steeply up between the northern edge of Dodd Wood and the wooded grounds of the Ravenstone Hotel.

Climb this path, bearing left, to reach a gate/stile leading onto the open fellside. Continue up the obvious path bearing leftwards along the edge of a wood. Ignore a narrower path forking right and continue on to where a cairn marks a path fork. Now take the right-hand path which twists steeply upwards to reach the crest of a ridge. Beyond this crest lies the bleak upland valley of Southerndale, dominated by the massive scree-capped dome of Skiddaw.

Turn right and follow the ridge, climbing towards the graceful and beckoning cone of Ullock Pike. From the summit of Ullock Pike the entire gleaming, yacht-speckled length of Bassenthwaite Lake is spread below. North-westerly the green Cumbrian flatlands and the grey Solway Firth stretch away to meet Scotland, whilst southwards a magnificent jumble of peaks are jammed between south-easterly Catstycam and south-westerly Whiteside.

Beyond Ullock Pike continue pleasantly along the grassy and slaty crest of Longside Edge. Compared to the Premier League ridges of Sharp, Striding, and Hall's Fell this is a Scunthorpe United kind of an 'edge'. Plain fare, but enjoyable for all that. It ends in a dip beyond which rises the heathery dome of Carlside. The path now edges leftwards along the rim of Southerndale, bypassing the summit of Carlside, to reach a grassy saddle below the south top of Skiddaw, crowned by tiny Carlside Tarn. Now climb the obvious path slanting left across vast scree slopes. This eventually swings right and steepens before emerging onto Skiddaw's

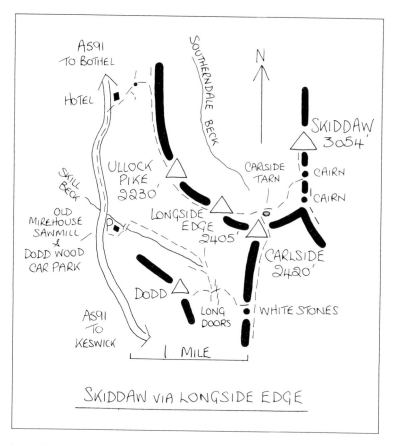

SKIDDAW VIA LONGSIDE EDGE

broad summit dome near the central of its three 'tops'. Turn left over this 'central top' into a dip then on up to the 'trig-point'.

The view from Skiddaw is remarkable more for its extent than its detail. It's an ideal location for the enthusiastic fell-spotter to attempt to orientate him or herself to all the splendid humpety and bumpety spread around and below. I'll presume to give you a couple of clues. Helvellyn is approximately south-south-east and Gable is approximately south-south-west. Skiddaw has long been a popular climb. A Bishop of Carlisle climbed it in 1684 and five years later a small observatory was set up on the summit. On the evening of August 21st, 1815, the Southeys and the Wordsworths and an entourage of friends and helpers lit a bonfire and had a 'knees-up' on the summit to celebrate the victory at Waterloo.

To descend, reverse your upward route back to Carlside Tarn. From here climb south-westerly and easily over slaty rocks to reach the summit cairn of Carlside. Beyond this follow a path bearing leftwards, south, which descends the fell's south ridge just below and to the left of its crest. Leftwards the ground falls steeply away into a gill, with the shapely outlier of Carsleddam rising across its depths. Beyond and below lie the roofs of Keswick, gleaming island-pocked Derwentwater, and the dark Jaws of Borrowdale. The path heads down towards the obvious natural feature of White Stones. At the White Stones turn right along a fainter path flanking across the heathery fellside. Below looms wooded Dodd. Shortly a path forks leftwards and down. Descend this to reach a stile in a fence leading onto the forest road crowning Long Doors, the narrow saddle dividing Carlside and Dodd.

Turn right and down the forest 'road' which splits at the head of Skill Beck. Take the 'road' leading down the right bank. Ignore any 'roads' or paths forking right but continue down, with Skill Beck below and to your left, to return to the car-park.

Blencathra via the Hall's Fell ridge

Blencathra – a lovely name for a magnificent mountain, although it's reputed to mean 'Peak of Devils'. It's a safe bet to be included in any Lakeland XI versus a World Mountain XI. The estimable Mr. Wainwright describes the Hall's Fell route as 'positively the finest way to any mountain top in the district'. With Sharp Edge just around the corner many, including myself, would be forced to disagree with him whilst still rating Hall's Fell very highly. Readers will find the ascent gives the a flavour of proper mountaineering minus the danger. Under snow and ice it can be a different story and an ice-axe, at least, should be carried. The ridge has the added bonus of finishing slap-bang up against the summit cairn. The Doddick Fell ridge gives similar but easier going and would be raved about if stuck onto a lump like Loadpot Hill. Such is the quality of Blencathra it has to take third place in the fell's splendid ridges. If you enjoy this walk next time try Sharp Edge.

Parking: On the A66 Penrith-Keswick, either in a lay-by on the south verge at Scales, or a lay-by on the north verge half-a-mile west. (GR 339267/344269).

ABOUT halfway between the lay-bys, leave the road by a path climbing between a red-porched cottage and Scales Farm to a gate. Beyond the gate, turn left alongside a wall to reach the rocky banks of Scaley Beck. Scramble across the beck and continue alongside the wall to a path fork. Take the left fork down to a gate. Pass through it and continue to a gate leading on to the banks of Doddick Gill. Cross the gill and continue alongside the wall to reach the weir at the foot of Gategill. Don't cross the weir, turn right and attack the path climbing steeply up the broad heathery base of Hall's Fell. This weir and the ruined building above it provide further evidence that Blencathra once attracted men more for the riches entombed in its slaty depths than the airy delights of its ridges. Mining began in the 16th century but the bonanza years were 1860 to 1900 when the Woodend Mine produced £120,000 of ore and employed around one hundred men and boys. Just over a thousand feet of steady plodding leads to where the ridge proper begins and the fun starts. Now half a mile of rocky, curving and crenellated ridge leads delightfully up to the summit cairn. On either hand the ground falls steeply away into the depths of Gate Gill and Doddick Gill. Beyond the latter rises the Doddick Fell ridge, your prospective way down. This upper section of Hall's Fell is sometimes called Narrow Edge. For those who find their

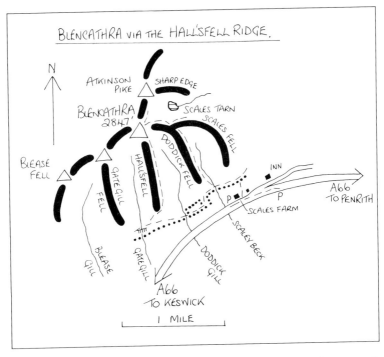

BLENCATHRA VIA THE HALL'SFELL RIDGE.

N

ATKINSON PIKE   SHARP EDGE

BLENCATHRA 2847'   SCALES TARN   SCALES FELL

DODDICK FELL

BLEASE FELL

GATE GILL FELL   HALLSFELL   INN

BLEASE GILL   GATEGILL   SCALES FARM   P   P   A66 TO PENRITH

DODDICK GILL   SCALEY BECK

A66 TO KESWICK

1 MILE

first sight of Narrow Edge intimidating be assured that a path wends its way round the rock towers. The true delight and achievement that this edge offers, however, is in attempting to stick as closely to the crest as possible.

Perched on the very rim of the massive Threlkeld flank, Blencathra's cairn overlooks a superb 'bird's-eye' view – the cream of it, in my opinion, above and between Thirlmere and Derwentwater. Arrayed here are the shapely cone of Gable with the brawny shoulders of Scafell Pike to its left. Leftwards still can be spotted the ubiquitous pyramid of Bowfell and the crumpled crest of neighbouring Crinkle Crags. See if you can spot the Castlerigg Stone Circle, below Derwentwater and the stark profile of Walla Crag.

To descend, bear right from the cairn, as you approached it, down a path that soon swings left. Leave it where cairns mark a path dropping away to your right. Follow this path down a steep grass slope which levels out onto an obvious ridge. This ridge falls away leftwards in easy angled grass but rightwards is rimmed with rock which plunges precipitously into the depths of Doddick Gill. Below the slope on your left the dark waters of Scales Tarn nestle under the slabby flanks and notched crest of Sharp Edge, Lakeland's premier ridge. Your path runs slightly below and behind the ridge's rocky rim. In a gap before the last rocky knobble a cairn marks the way down onto the Doddick Fell ridge.

Turn down into the gap where the path bears leftwards along the base of a rocky tower to where the ridge becomes more defined. The path is well-worn and the ridge offers no problems save two small rocky steps which are easily negotiated. Below the last step the ridge levels out before rising slightly again. Look for a cairn marking the start of a path forking left and down into the ravine of Scaley Beck. Follow this path down to join your outward path just above Scaley Beck. Cross the beck and return to your car.

A Derwentwater Walkabout

A longish but amiable and entertaining walk amidst compelling scenery. Can equally be started from Keswick or any point on the lakeshore. Can be done leisurely, pausing en route for picnics or swims, or organised to arrive in Keswick for lunch, liquid or otherwise. It can be done in sections, walking from landing stage to landing stage and taking advantage of the regular motor launch service.

Parking: (for example). The National Trust 'Kettlewell' car park on Derwentwater's eastern shore, just over 2½ miles from Keswick, and just over half a mile past the Watendlath turn-off, along the Borrowdale road, B5289. (GR 267196).

LEAVE the car park and head north, towards Keswick, along the lakeshore. The path becomes grassier as it proceeds around the next point and into Barrow Bay, overlooked by tree-plumed Walla Crag and starker, steeper Falcon Crag. The path passes behind a landing stage then follows a strip of shore squeezed between lake and road before rounding a wooded promontory and entering Calf Close Bay. The swing around Calf Close Bay leads onto a further wooded cape pointing at tiny Rampsholme Island, reputedly named after the 'ramp' or wild garlic which grew (or grows?) there. Across the lake the Coledale fells are moving into view behind the slowly receding Catbells. Grisedale Pike's elegant cone overlooks lowly Barrow but as always cocky Causey Pike attempts to steal the show.

When Stable Hills House is reached the path veers away from the lake to a gate leading onto a rough track. Turn left. Above the woods ahead looms the broad, rounded Blease Fell flank of Blencathra. As the track curves right a gate will be seen below on the edge of a wood. Go down and through this to follow a path around the edge of The Ings, a National Trust plantation, to eventually emerge on the shore of Strandshag Bay. The mouth of this bay is guarded by Lord's Island, once a residence of the ill-fated Jacobite Earls of Derwentwater. When the wooded promontory of Friar's Crag is approached take a path forking left and climb up and out to its point. Ruskin, whose memorial crowns Friar's Crag, maintained the view from it was the fifth finest in Europe. The postcards and the gawking thousands have not extinguished the magic of the limpid water, the dark, moored islands, and the subtly carved and coloured fells. Anchored almost alongside Friar's Crag

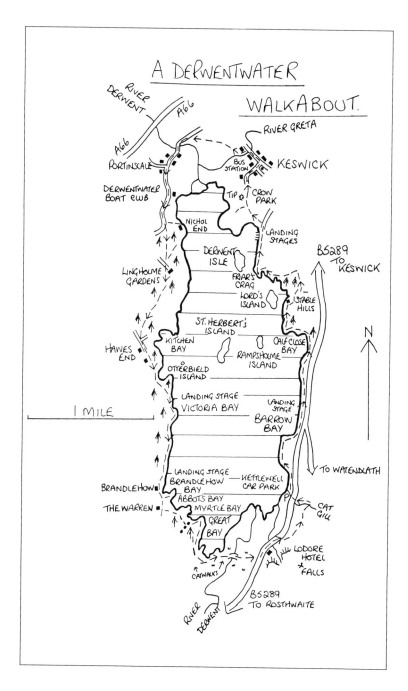

is large, timbered Derwent Isle, once the temporary haven for sixteenth-century German miners when the natives became a little restless (see Walk 32). It was also once the home of the eighteenth-century entrepreneur and showman Joseph Pocklington who organised mock sea-battles on Derwentwater.

Return along the point and follow the road running past the boat landing stages. Climb the rise beyond these and look for a gate in the railings on your left leading into Crow Park. Pass through this and walk rightwards across the slope of the park, away from the path leading to Isthmus Bay, to reach and pass through a gate leading onto a road close to the town rubbish dump. Turn right now and follow the road past caravan sites, the rugby club, a supermarket and shops, to join the main street. Turn left. After crossing a bridge over the River Greta turn left at a footpath sign 'Portinscale'. Shortly this path forks; bear right across fields to join a road. Turn left. Ahead now the elegant cones and domes of the Coledale fells rise above the hamlet of Portinscale.

Follow the road and cross an elegantly arched footbridge over the River Derwent. Continue up the road ahead, passing the Derwentwater Hotel, to a T junction. Turn left and follow the road, passing the Derwentwater Boat Club. Shortly after passing the Derwent Bank Guest House look for a lane on your left signposted 'Catbells by Nichol End, Lingholme, Hawes End'. Ignore this and continue on, passing the entrance to 'Fawe Park', to shortly reach a gap in the hedge to your left signposted 'Footpath to Brandlehow'. Go through the gap and climb the path through woods then down to a junction of paths near a wall. Continue alongside the wall to join a road near the entrance to Lingholme Gardens.

Go through a gate to the right of the entrance signposted 'Footpath to Brandlehow and the Lake'. The path now goes through woodland to reach a gate signposted 'Public Footpath' on the edge of a field. Cross the field, with the Catbells looming above the trees ahead and Causey Pike to the right. The path goes through a gate, crosses a clapper-bridge over a beck, and climbs up through trees to emerge onto a junction of roads and paths. Take the road signposted 'Hawes End' and 'Boat Landing'. Walk down the road (drive) to pass to the left of the house at Hawes End to reach a gate. Pass through this and follow a path down a field, passing close to the shore of Otterbield Bay, to reach a gate in a fence. Barely breaking the surface of the bay is tiny Otterbield Island, with larger, wooded, St. Herbert's Isle looming beyond. The latter was the seventh-century hermitage of a friend and disciple of the Northumbrian saint, St. Cuthbert.

Beyond the gate the path bears left through a muddy gap, between woods. Shortly the shore of Victoria Bay is reached near a landing stage. Now about a mile of delightful walking follows, with the path twisting and turning along the wooded and rocky shore of the lake. When the Brandlehow landing stage is passed the path climbs up slate steps onto the crest of an old spoil heap. A huge water-wheel once trundled noisily on the shore of Brandlehow Bay, pumping water out of Brandley Mine whose shafts went deep into the rocky vitals of the Catbells. Postlethwaite, whose 'Mines and Mining in the English Lake District' is a classic, states that as well as lead and copper traces of gold were discovered here.

After passing through a gate on the edge of the wood turn left, alongside a wall, then right to pass between a boathouse and white-walled 'Brandlehow' to reach a gate. Beyond this follow a track to a T junction. Turn right and follow the track to a gate, passing 'The Warren'. Beyond the gate is a National Trust sign 'Manesty Wood' and to the left a sign 'Footpath to Lodore'. Follow the latter and a path twisting through the woods fringing the shores of Abbot's Bay and Myrtle Bay to reach a gate in a wall. Beyond this, either turn left along the wall to reach the lakeshore and turn right along it, around Great Bay, or head diagonally leftwards across the open heath, bearing just to the right of woods. Both routes eventually merge into a path heading leftwards across marshy ground towards the distant white-walled Lodore Hotel. Soon wooden catwalks lead to a footbridge over the River Derwent. Continue on to a stile leading onto the Borrowdale road. Turn left. A couple of hundred yards past the Lodore Hotel a gap in the wall on your right leads onto a path bearing left through the woods and parallel to the road. This leads to a footbridge over Cat Gill. Cross this and turn left to follow the beck down a gap in a wall opposite your car park.

Walla Crag and Ashness Bridge

*A delightful and amiable walk that constantly offers scenes of un-
surpassed Lakeland splendour. An ideal outing for the walker-cum-
birdwatcher, photographer, painter, or for a family party – or for a
hot leisurely day when a book is stuffed into the pack along with the
sandwiches. The last time my wife and I did this walk we sat on a
grassy shelf high above Ashness Bridge eating our lunch and reading
before both quietly 'zonking-out' in a Borrowdale siesta.*

*Parking: From Keswick take the Borrowdale road, B5289, for
around a mile and a half before turning left at the first 'National
Trust, Free Car Park' sign into Great Wood, under the shadow of
the towering tree-draped Walla Crag. (GR 272213).*

LEAVE the rear of the car-park by the stile signposted 'Public
Footpath to Walla Crag-Ashness Bridge'. Follow the path rightwards to a junction signposted '◁ Walla Crag-Ashness Bridge ▷'.
Turn left here. This path climbs gradually through thick woodland
for nearly a mile. There are tantalising glimpses of Walla Crag
looming above the trees on your right and, frustratingly, moving
behind. Do not worry, you are on the right path. When the path
forks follow the right-hand fork to reach a stile on the edge of
woods. Skiddaw and its shapely acolytes fill the sky ahead. From
left to right are wooded Dodd, rounded Carlside, the graceful
cones of Skiddaw and Low Man, and the flattened dome of
Lonscale Fell. Below, Derwentwater and Bassenthwaite Lake lead
the eye, given a clear day, to the distant Solway Firth. Across
Derwentwater rise the precise pyramid of Grisedale Pike, burly
Crag Hill, and the cocky dimples of Causey Pike.

Cross the stile and follow a path between a fence and wall to a
junction with a path on the right bank of Brockle Beck. Turn right
and follow this path up the beck to a stile. Cross the stile and
continue to a footbridge over the beck. Cross this to a gate leading
onto a tarmac lane. Turn right. When the lane forks near Rakefoot
Farm take the right fork, signposted 'Walla Crag'. This leads to a
footbridge leading back across Brockle Beck. Cross this and turn
left up a path climbing alongside a wall to a gate-stile. Beyond this
continue alongside the wall which shortly swings right. The metal
grid embedded in the ground around here was apparently laid
down when this was a tank training area during World War Two.
Eventually the angle eases and the flat summit of Walla Crag rises
ahead. Pleasant walking across springy turf leads to a gate in a wall

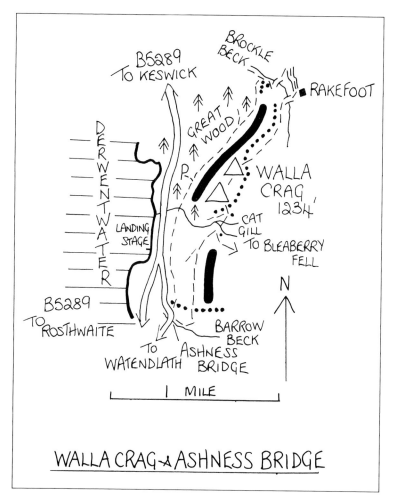

WALLA CRAG → ASHNESS BRIDGE

leading onto the slabby northern, and higher, summit of Walla Crag. The fell's twin tops are divided by a shallow grassy cleft running down into the head of Lady's Rake, an obvious gully splitting the crag when seen from below.

The view from either top is superb. Derwentwater with its sylvan islands (see Walk 28 for details) and headlands spreads below. In the high season its gleaming surface is scattered with a dressing of rowing boats, sailing craft and the arrowing wakes of the ubiquitous motor launches. Across the lake rise the fells of Newlands and Coledale. On his first sight of them Coleridge wrote, 'before me there is a great Camp of Mountains – each

Mountain is a Giant's Tent – and how the light streams from them – and the shadows that travel upon them.' From Walla Crag this is a delightfully perceptive description. Follow the path along the rim of the crag, across the head of Lady's Rake, on to the south summit.

To continue go beyond the cairn on the south summit and through a gate in a wall. Just beyond the gate a cairn marks a junction of green grassy paths. Follow the left, upper, fork. The dark heathery summit away to your left is Bleaberry Fell. Ahead King's How and Castle Crag thrust above the tree-choked Jaws of Borrowdale with knobbly Glaramara and smooth and shapely (from this angle) Gable rising beyond. Above Glaramara and left of Gable are the more distant humps of Great End and Scafell Pike. Soon a small cairn marks another fork. Keep to the right-hand and more worn path which drops down to cross the tributary becks of Cat Gill. Glance back over your right shoulder for an interesting prospect of the islands and headlands of Derwentwater in verdant echelon towards Keswick. Your path slants down across the head of Cat Gill's combe and onto a wide grassy shelf. This shelf runs above Falcon Crag and below terraces of small broken crags. Follow it. Away across Derwentwater, Causey Pike has transformed itself into an elegant Lakeland Matterhorn. When the path forks near the rim of the shelf follow the left-hand path to a stile over a wall. Beyond this follow a path across the fellside to reach the edge of Barrow Beck. Walk downstream to Ashness Bridge and its splendid backcloth of lake and fell. Enough film must have been exposed hereabouts to keep a brigade of Japanese tourists happy for a six month holiday.

Cross the bridge and walk down the road to shortly see a path branching right signposted 'Great Wood and Keswick'. Follow this to cross a stile. The path twists amiably across the fellside towards the stark profile of Falcon Crag. At a fork carry straight on; shortly a fingerpost points right. Falcon Crag is split into an upper and lower crag and as you pass below its surprisingly colourful slabs and overhangs you may spot a gymnastic 'crag-rat' or two in action. When the path forks beyond Falcon Crag continue straight ahead towards the wall guarding the edge of Great Wood. Turn right up alongside the wall and then left across a footbridge spanning Cat Gill. Follow the path beyond to shortly reach your car.

NEWLANDS

Barrow, Stile End and Outerside

This fine trio of shapely minor fells deserve far more attention than they appear to attract. Perhaps their fault lies in rising in the shadow of one of Lakeland's 'classic' horseshoes. Nevertheless they provide an enjoyable expedition, giving relatively easy walking and varied and compelling views.

Parking: From Keswick head for Braithwaite via the B5289, A66 and B5292. In Braithwaite follow the 'Newlands' signs leftwards over the narrow bridge. Ignore the fork 'Swinside' and when the wood on your right falls away, beyond a cattle grid, look for a parking space on the grass verge on your right. (GR 234224)

WALK up the road, past a memorial seat, to where a path sign-posted 'Public Bridleway – Braithwaite' slants up the fellside to your right. Follow this. When Braithwaite comes into view below and ahead, with Bassenthwaite Lake gleaming beyond, the path forks. Follow the upper path to a junction with the path climbing Barrow's north-east ridge. Turn left up this. A straightforward and grassy plod now leads to a dip bearing traces of past mining. Barrow's narrow and heathery summit beckons ahead with Causey Pike's dimpled crest and the notched ridge of Scar Crags looming above and beyond. The gap to the right of Scar Crags is Sail Hause, dominated by the dome of Sail. To your right, Stile End and Outerside beckon in the foreground. Beyond them bulky Crag Hill and graceful Grisedale Pike, divided by the saddle of Coledale Hause, dominate the head of Coledale. The Cistercian monks of the 14th century drained 'Husaker Tarn' in order to create their 'Neulandes'. The name and the site linger on in Uzzicar Farm at the foot of the steep slope to your left.

From Barrow top the path bears right and down into the heathery saddle of Barrow Door. A path linking Braithwaite and Stonycroft Gill crosses this saddle. Cross this path and climb rightwards up onto the rounded summit of Stile End, the most innocuous of your trio. From Stile End head south-westerly across the boggy saddle of Low Moss towards the inviting shape of Outerside. The path is indistinct at times but improves as Outerside is approached. A final steep pull brings you onto the pleasant grassy summit ridge crowned by a cairn at its far end.

Because it is tucked deep into the heart of the Coledale Horse-

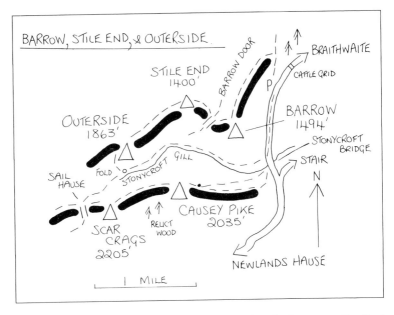

BARROW, STILE END, & OUTERSIDE

STILE END 1400'

BARROW DOOR

BRAITHWAITE

CATTLE GRID

P

OUTERSIDE 1863'

BARROW 1494'

STONYCROFT BRIDGE

STAIR

STONYCROFT GILL

FOLD

SAIL HAUSE

N

SCAR CRAGS 2205'

RELICT WOOD

CAUSEY PIKE 2035'

NEWLANDS HAUSE

1 MILE

shoe the views from Outerside are restricted. I personally find compensation in the intimate detail revealed of the mountain architecture of its loftier neighbours, particularly the rugged north-east flank of Crag Hill looming ahead. Close inspection of this face will reveal a broad rocky rib running up the centre of it, and from the foot of this rib a natural shelf climbing diagonally rightwards to an obvious nick in the skyline. Mr. Wainwright has christened the rib 'Tower Ridge' and the natural line 'Shelf Route'. Both are entertaining, especially under snow. Below the western rim of Outerside lie the ramshackle buildings of Force Crag Mine. Barytes was mined here and the mine has been sporadically operational until quite recently. Above the buildings Pudding Beck spills cream-ily over vertiginous and vegetated Force Crag.

Now head down leftwards, south, to join, near a sheepfold, the rough former mining track that climbs out of Stonycroft Gill and ultimately up onto Sail Hause. If you are still feeling energetic at this point and fancy 'bagging' Scar Crags and Causey Pike turn right and follow this track up to Sail Hause. Turn left here up onto the broad boggy ridge leading to the summit of Scar Crags. Beyond, the ridge dips modestly before rising again to form the bumpety ridge whose final rocky burp is the summit of Causey Pike – with its superb views. The descent begins with a steepish rocky scramble but easier ground is soon reached followed by a cairned fork in the path. Left is easier, right more interesting, both lead down to Stonycroft Bridge and the road.

Otherwise, turn left and follow the miners track down Stonycroft Gill. Traces of former mining can be found along the banks of the gill and one ancient mining tragedy here is reputed to have entombed a whole shift. Just above Stoneycroft Bridge the path forks. Take the left-hand path which brings you out onto the Newlands road a little nearer your car. Walk left along the road below the eroded eastern flank of Barrow, once extensively mined.

Knott Rigg and Ard Crags

A fine and easily accessible walk that deserves greater popularity. Has a steep start and a steep finish but the walking in between is so amiable and enjoyable that you should have plenty of energy left.

Parking: Follow the directions for Walk 30 but then continue up the Newlands road for a further 4½ miles to park on the summit of Newlands Hause. (GR 193176).

NEARBY Moss Force, spilling down a rocky spur of Robinson, is a popular tourist attraction. You can make it the scenic 'hors-d'oeuvre' or 'dessert' to your main course. Climb the steep and well-worn path from the northern verge up to the summit ridge of Knott Rigg. To your left, as you climb, the graceful outlines of Whiteless Pike and Wandope tower above the depths of Sail Beck. To your right, across Newlands Hause, looms the rugged bulk of Robinson. Pause and turn around to see below you the roofs of Buttermere village and a dark glinting segment of Crummock Water below the rounded skyline of Red Pike, Starling Dod and Great Borne, with Sour Milk Gill lacing a silvery thread down Red Pike's sombre skirt of trees. By the time you have reached the crest of the ridge High Stile and High Crag have risen above the flanks of Robinson to link rocky arms with Red Pike. Looming behind them is the high dome of Pillar.

You now step onto an elegant grassy ridge which eventually becomes broader and a trifle squelchier before reaching Knott Rigg's summit cairn. Ahead now the dimpled summit of Causey Pike peeps over Ard Crags, your next objective. Leftwards from Causey Pike, Scar Crags, Sail, Crag Hill and Wandope curve and climb around and above you. The constant and almost overpowering loom of this massive mountain wall, rough-sculpted by glaciers, weather and time, is for me one of the most fascinating aspects of this walk. Below, the pastoral splendour of Newlands stretches away towards Derwentwater and guardian Blencathra. To your right Hindscarth rises into view behind Robinson.

From Knott Rigg summit a subsidiary spur branches eastwards before turning north-easterly and steeply down to meet the Newlands road near Keskadale Farm and separated from the main ridge by the ravine of Ill Gill. The plantation of trees clinging to the northern wall of Ill Gill just above Keskadale Farm are the Keskadale Oaks, reputedly one of Lakeland's surviving areas of relict or original woodland.

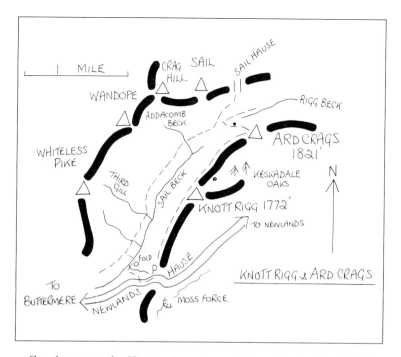

Continue past the Knott Rigg cairn and down to a hollow holding a small pond. Soon the ground narrows again and a heathery ridge leads up to the summit of Ard Crags, the high point of the walk. To the right now the view has opened up to include Dalehead, the highest peak of the classic Newlands Horseshoe. Framed in the gap to the left of Dalehead are the craggy knobbles of Combe Head and Glaramara, with bluff High Raise and the cone of Pike O'Stickle rising beyond. Scafell Pike and Gable can be seen in the gap between Hindscarth and Robinson. Leftwards, across the depths of Rigg Beck, the Birk Rigg Oaks, a further threadbare remnant of woody history, fight for foothold on the steep flank of Scar Crags.

Just over four hundred feet below and to the left of the Ard Crags summit cairn lies the grassy saddle that is the watershed of the Sail and Rigg becks. Now leave the ridge and descend steepish, pathless, but safe grass to reach this saddle, which is crowned by a small cairn. Cross the saddle near the cairn and climb a short way up the opposite slope to join a crossing path. This path links Newlands with Buttermere through the valleys of the Rigg and Sail becks – a splendid walker's route that avoids the hard tarmac, exhaust fumes and grinding gears of Newlands Hause. Turn left.

The path leaves the saddle to slant gradually down across the southern flank of Sail. Shortly a path descending from Sail Hause joins in on your right. This return down Sail Beck can be magnificent on a summer evening with the crests haloed in a blaze of gold and a silent silver thread of beck spilling over the high rim of Addacomb Hole. Addacomb Beck is crossed near old mine workings and the path now slants gradually down across the flank of Wandope to reach and cross Third Gill. A similar line is then followed across Bleak Rigg to reach and cross an un-named beck and emerge onto the flank of Whiteless Breast. Below and ahead now a sheepfold will be seen on the far bank of Sail Beck near its junction with Swinside Gill. Above the fold will also be seen the road slanting up to Newlands Hause. When convenient head down towards the fold and across Sail Beck. Once on the far bank walk past the fold, cross Swinside Gill and climb a faint path that slants leftwards and then directly up to reach the road. Turn left up the road to shortly reach your car.

The Newlands Trio

When Coleridge first saw the Newlands and Coledale fells from Keswick he described them as 'a great Camp of Mountains – each Mountain is a Giant's Tent'. Two of the most shapely of these 'tents' are Robinson and Hindscarth. The walk described below takes in these two and their more retiring but higher neighbour Dalehead. The walk ends with exploration of the old workings of an Elizabethan Klondike.

Parking: Just beyond Littletown in the Newlands Valley on the grass verges at the foot of a steep hill near a bridge over the Newlands Beck. (GR 233195). Space is limited, get there early.

GO over the bridge and turn left through the gate signposted 'Newlands Church and High Snab'. Walk past the church and follow the tarmac road ahead, climbing past the road end to High Snab to reach and pass Low High Snab Farm. Go through two gates into a grassy lane. Just beyond where the right wall turns uphill the path forks. Take the right fork which climbs steeply up the fellside to reach the grassy crest of High Snab Bank. Here you are rewarded for your efforts by a splendid view of the massive, eroded southern flanks of Crag Hill, Wandope, Whiteless Pike and Grasmoor across the depths of Keskadale. Tucked into a fold of modest Ard Crags, above Keskadale Farm, are the Keskadale Oaks (see Walk 31).

High Snab abuts Robinson proper where two pitches of slabby scrambling add a smidgin of 'mountaineering' to the ascent. Down to your left Scope Beck spills creamily out of the high valley of Little Dale towards the dark depths of a tiny reservoir constructed to provide power for one of Newland's many defunct mines. Above the scrambling the path climbs steeply up a broad ridge with a craggy drop to its right. The summit dome is reached near a large cairn. Easy walking south-westerly across the broad summit for around a third of a mile reaches the summit cairn perched on a slaty fin of rock. Robinson was named after a local Tudor entrepreneur who was quick to grasp the opportunities offered by the dissolution of the monasteries, for the monks held much of Lakeland. The broad summit dome obstructs the valley views but the surrounding display of fells is excellent – particularly bluff King Grasmoor and his shapely acolytes across the depths of Newlands Hause, and the superb triumvirate of Red Pike, High Stile and High Crag towering above dark, glinting Buttermere. A bonus on a clear day is the northern prow of the Isle of Man thrusting around the high shoulder of Red Pike.

Now head south to meet a wooden fence. Follow it down and across the high grassy saddle at the head of Little Dale, the bare upland valley dividing Robinson from Hindscarth. The wooden fence soon turns away but the rusting remnants of the old iron boundary fence now accompany the path on the steep climb up onto the broad grassy summit ridge of Hindscarth. Turn left now and follow this ridge in a gentle climb of just under half a mile to reach the summit cairn. Just beyond and below this cairn is a fine windbreak. If exhaustion or deteriorating weather at this point hint that your walk should be curtailed, continue north-north-east down past the windbreak into a hollow holding a small tarn. Beyond this a short climb leads onto the elegant High Crags ridge which eventually drops steeply down to Low Snab Farm. This is an entertaining alternative walk as well as an escape route.

Otherwise, return along the summit ridge to the old fence posts and path and follow both leftwards, south-easterly, into a dip and up onto the somewhat grandiosely christened Hindscarth Edge. Although rocky and falling away steeply on either flank this is yet another Third Division (Northern) kind of an 'edge'. From it glance over your right shoulder for a fine full-length view of Buttermere. Hindscarth Edge and its bristle of rusty fence posts leads to the elegant cairn balanced on the precipitous northern rim of Dalehead, the high point of your walk.

Stand close to it and dizzy fathoms of Lakeland air separate your toe caps from the valley floor. Below, the green corridor of Newlands, fenced by the darker contours of High Spy and Maiden Moor, stretches away towards distant Derwentwater and the comfortable curves of Skiddaw. Descend eastwards along the northern rim of Dalehead. Around two hundred feet below the summit look for a cairn marking a path slanting leftwards onto the north face. This descends diagonally and delightfully across the steep rough fellside, passing an old mine shaft, to reach the ruins of an old mine building. Pass to the left of the ruin and across slabby rocks to a cairn. Beyond this a hollowed grassy path zig-zags downwards. This is an old 'sledgate' down which ore was once carried on sleds or 'trailbarrows', the miners running down before them like a horse. This path eventually slants leftwards across the rocky ravine of Far Tongue Gill, then passes under a small spoil heap before heading down towards Newlands Beck. At a junction turn left along a fainter path heading across the fellside. This crosses Near Tongue Gill then heads towards the foot of the rocky outcrop of Squat Knotts. Beyond Squat Knotts the path temporarily disappears in a patch of boggy ground. Cross this and head for the left-hand corner of the wall blocking the valley ahead to pick up the path again. Follow it, alongside a wall, to eventually reach the foot of the massive spoil heaps of the old Goldscope Mine.

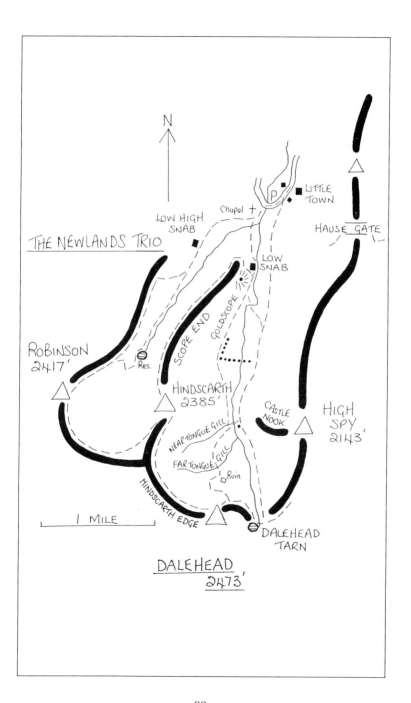

N

LITTLE TOWN

P

Chapel

LOW HIGH SNAB

THE NEWLANDS TRIO

HAUSE GATE

LOW SNAB

GOLDSCOPE

SCOPE END

ROBINSON
2417'

Res.

HINDSCARTH
2385'

CASTLE NOOK

HIGH SPY
2143'

NEAR TONGUE GILL

FAR TONGUE GILL

Ruin

HINDSCARTH EDGE

1 MILE

DALEHEAD TARN

DALEHEAD
2473'

The 16th century emigrant German miners brought over to unearth the riches of Newlands christened it 'Gottesgab' or 'God's Gift'. With copper and lead veins nine and thirteen feet thick it was reported as 'the best in England'. Reputedly traces of gold were also found. These skilled, travelled and highly paid foreigners were an attraction for local girls, causing some disenchantment amongst Tudor Cumbrian males. There were ugly scenes and at least one murder, and for a while the Germans were lodged on Derwent Isle for their own safety. Eventually they became accepted and intermarried. Beck, Moser, Calvert, Raisley and Caryus are just a handful of the anglicised German names surviving in Cumbria.

The 'adits' or levels, one above the other, cut deeply into the flank of Scope End. These are potentially dangerous places. After a circumspect peek, or couple of steps, into their stygian gloom retire down to Low Snab Farm to buy a fortifying 'cuppa'. Afterwards, continue down the farm track to a junction with your outward route near Newlands Church.

Caution
Should the path slanting down the steep north flank of Dalehead be icy, or snow-covered, it would be advisable, if you are not suitably equipped, to continue down the popular route to Dalehead Tarn. Walk to the left of the tarn to pass a sheepfold under a small crag. Then turn left and down, between outcrops, to cross the infant Newlands Beck. Once across, turn left and follow the path alongside the beck down into the valley. After rounding the rocky spur of Castle Nook the path becomes a broad track which eventually reaches the road near the crest of the hill above your car. Should you wish, however, to explore the environs of Goldscope Mine and have a 'cuppa' at Low Snab Farm, leave the above path when opposite Near Tongue Gill, cross the Newlands Beck, and follow the original directions as given from the foot of Near Tongue Gill.

BORROWDALE

Castle Crag

The Jaws of Borrowdale, where the valley's tree-draped and crag-scabbed flanks squeeze in upon the pellucid Derwent, typifies Borrowdale scenery in the hearts and minds of many Lakeland enthusiasts. Here is an opportunity to explore this rugged but lovely defile.

Parking: Rosthwaite village car park (GR 257148)

LEAVE the car park, turn right, and follow the lane to Yew Tree Farm. Walk past the farm and into a walled lane signposted 'Grange'. This leads to the bank of the River Derwent near stepping stones. Ignore these and continue along the river bank to a bridge, New Bridge. Cross this, turn right, and follow a further 'Grange' sign to a pair of gates. (If the flow allows it, and you fancy it, cross the stones and turn right along the far bank to reach these gates.) Go through the right-hand gate and follow the path along the river bank. After crossing a tributary beck by a clapper-bridge (stone slabs spanning a beck), the path swings left. When it begins to turn right, towards a wood, a gate will be seen on your left with a path climbing steeply up the fellside beyond it. Pass through this gate and begin to climb.

A steep pull leads to a gate, and on to a further gate, and beyond that to a stile over a wall. Beyond this stile, framed between magnificent Scot's pines, Castle Crag and opposing Goat Crag spill crag, scree and boulder into a rugged gorge. Cross the stile and climb the path twisting steeply up the tumbled slate hacked out of the very summit of the fell to reach the topmost rocks which bear a memorial tablet to Borrowdale men who fell in the Great War.

The rugged incisors of the 'Jaws of Borrowdale', nipping in, restrict the views from Castle Crag. Nevertheless, as you step up onto the summit you are greeted by a fine 'surprise' view north-wards of Derwentwater backed by the broad maternal skirts of Skiddaw. Southwards, Glaramara is predominant, a sprawling armchair of a fell with Thornthwaite Fell and Rosthwaite Cam forming bumpy armrests to the uncomfortable seat of Combe Gill, knobbly with drumlins like faulty springs.

There are many Castle 'crags', 'hows', 'heads', and 'rocks' in Lakeland. Invariably, they are isolated rocky hillocks dominating

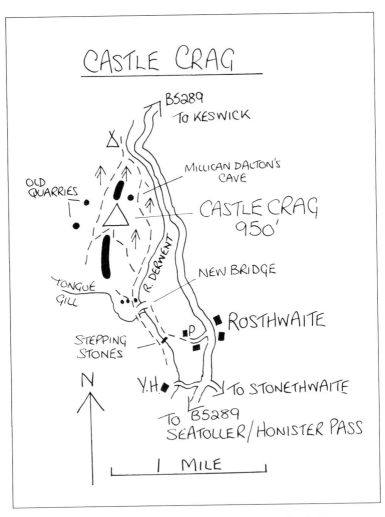

CASTLE CRAG

B5289
TO KESWICK

MILLICAN DALTON'S
CAVE

OLD
QUARRIES

CASTLE CRAG
950'

R. DERWENT

NEW BRIDGE

TONGUE
GILL

ROSTHWAITE

STEPPING
STONES

P

N

Y.H.

TO STONETHWAITE

TO B5289
SEATOLLER/HONISTER PASS

1 MILE

a valley mouth or the foot of a pass. Undoubtedly their common name springs from a time when they were look-outs or forts defended by primitive earthworks. When standing on the airy crest of Castle Crag it is easy to visualise how effectively it would fulfil either role.

Return down to the stile. Just before reaching it, turn diagonally down to your right to a stile in a fence. Cross this and descend the wooden steps beyond. Now bear left and down to pass through a gap in a wall before veering right to join an old quarry track on the bouldery floor of the ravine dividing Castle Crag and Goat Crag.

Turn right and descend this track, eventually into and through woodland, to reach the bank of the Derwent once again.

Turn right, upstream, and follow a path signposted 'Rosthwaite' along the wooded banks of the river. This section of the walk is delightful. The tree-shaded river runs particularly clear and calm here, inviting you to swim or picnic – given the weather. Presently the path climbs away from the river before turning left through a gap in a wall. Then it twists and undulates through boggy patches and around rocky hummocks before descending and passing through a gap in a further wall. Beyond this slate spoil heaps rise to your right. An opening in the slate leads to an old quarry spanned by a massive rock archway. In the thirties an eccentric Englishman, 'Millican Dalton, Professor of Adventure, Camping Holidays, Mountaineering, Rapid Shooting, Rafting and Hairbreadth Escapes', lived for many years in a cave on Castle Crag. Dalton, an educated man, threw up a business career to become a professional adventurer. He led parties climbing in Lakeland and the Alps. On a raft made of logs, tin cans and other junk he used to shoot the Derwent rapids. He died in 1947, aged eighty, apparently none the worse for his hard living.

Continue along the path to reach a fork. Turn right, following yellow waymarkers, along the base of small crags to shortly reach a gate at the edge of the woods. Just beyond this a junction is made with your outward route.

Langstrath

An amiable walk that takes you deep into the heart of one of Lakeland's loveliest upland valleys. Rugged mountainsides rise on either hand and the Langstrath Beck strings many splendid cascades and bathing pools along its meandering length. Black Moss Pot must take the crown for Lakeland's finest pool. The Grasmere artist W. Heaton-Cooper has painted it, which must bestow the aesthetic accolade.

Parking: Take the 'Stonethwaite' turn-off off the 'Borrowdale Road', the B5289. Follow this past a terrace of houses and a school. Park in a lay-by on the right of the lane leading to Stonethwaite, or by the telephone box in the hamlet itself. (GR 261139).

WALK through the hamlet and up the rough track beyond. In the 13th century Stonethwaite was a thriving 'vaccary' (a lovely word), or dairy farm, held by the Cistercians. Continue past the entrance to the campsite. Ahead, the valley is dominated by the stark profile of Eagle Crag. The lane bends left around a building piquantly named Alisongrass Hoghouse. Shortly beyond this the left wall turns away. Turn left here and follow a path across the grass to the rocky rim of Galleny Force. Bear right, along the edge of the beck, and cross a stile to emerge onto a promontory overlooking the confluence of Langstrath Beck, Greenup Gill and Seathwaite Beck. This area is known as Smithymire Island. This name echoes the time when it was the site of a medieval iron foundry or 'bloomery' worked by the Cistercians. The ore was packed out of Eskdale over the Ure, or Ore, gap, between Bowfell and Esk Pike, and down into Langstrath. To the untutored eye, like mine, the only visible evidence is the areas of scorched earth.

Follow the bank of Langstrath Beck around to a stile in a fence and beyond this turn left to rejoin the rough track. Continue along this, presently passing and ignoring a footbridge over the Langstrath Beck. Continue along the right bank. Ahead, the big crag dominating the left flank of the valley is Sergeant's Crag, easily recognised by the obvious dark cleft of Sergeant's Crag Gully, first climbed in 1893. The walls on either side of you eventually disappear, but the track continues on to reach a gate in a sheepfold close to the beck. Climb the stile to the right of the gate then turn left beyond the sheepfold on to the rocks rimming Black Moss Pot – the most illustrious of Lakeland's mountain pools. The path now veers away from the beck across grassy flats, before crossing rocky ground at

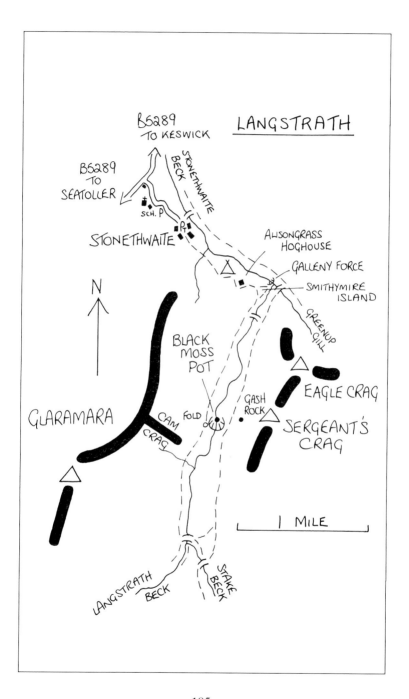

the foot of Cam Crag Ridge. The broad broken buttresses and pallid slabs of Cam Crag ridge provide a delightful 'scramble' that adds spice to an ascent of Glaramara from Langstrath. Continue up the valley to reach a footbridge over the Langstrath Beck beyond yet another fine pool and just before its junction with Stake Beck. Cross this bridge to begin your return route. Upper Langstrath, more sinuous and lonely but less ruggedly scarped, curves away to your right for two more miles, before ending in the dark rocky cleft of Allen Crags Gill.

Beyond the bridge a path climbs diagonally right towards a higher bridge crossing Stake Beck and ultimately to Stake Pass and Langdale. Stake Pass is an ancient Lakeland mountain highway. The Borrowdale Cistercians used to pack wool-clips and salt from their Manesty spring over it to the mother house. After the Reformation wool still went out to Kendal and timber and charcoal came back to feed Hochstetter's smelters; also feather beds, fine linen and wine to please his German miners and turn the heads of Cumbrian girls.

Cross the bridge and head straight up the fellside to join a path flanking across from the Stake Beck bridge. Now turn left. Just over a mile down valley a stile crosses a wall. Beyond it diverge left to peep, or dive, once more into Black Moss Pot. Shortly beyond Black Moss the path wends between piled boulders overlooked by a fissured monolith that old guide books term Gash Rock. Again ignore the lower footbridge across the Langstrath Beck, when reached, and continue along the right bank to reach and cross a footbridge over Greenup Gill opposite Smithymire Island. Beyond this a stile leads onto the stony Greenup Edge path, yet another ancient mountain trade route. Turn left down this. Just under a mile of easy walking brings a junction with a path leading leftwards, onto and across Stonethwaite Bridge and so back to your car.

Great Gable via Gillercombe

Great Gable, or Gable as it is more affectionately known, was one of my first Lakeland fells and has rewarded me since with many great days of climbing, scrambling and walking. If it is possible to apply that much misused word 'charisma' to a natural object, then Gable's bouldery dome and sanguine pinnacles and scree chutes reek with it. Gable turns its back on Borrowdale, being largely hidden from the valley by its outliers Base Brown and Green Gable. Nevertheless Seathwaite is the starting point for two amiable and popular routes up the mountain. The route described below combines both in an interesting and rewarding walk.

Parking: On the grass verges of the road leading to Seathwaite Farm. (GR 235123).

WALK up into Seathwaite Farm yard and turn right under the archway. Follow the lane to the footbridge over the infant Derwent. Above you Sour Milk Gill cascades down a thousand feet of pallid slabs and water-worn grooves. Away to its right a series of greyish spoil heaps blotch the rich green fellside. They disclose the shafts of the defunct Seathwaite Wadd Mine. Wadd, or graphite, was a valuable commodity in the 17th and 18th centuries. It could be used for multifarious purposes, ranging from the casting of round-shot to the easing of gallstone pain. The miners were searched after every shift and at night armed guards patrolled the site. Wadd convoys had an armed escort through the fell country until they reached Kendal. There is a theory that a touch more heat during the geological mix and it could have been diamonds not wadd mined at Seathwaite. Then what a different tale the history of Lakeland might have been!

Beyond the footbridge head up leftwards towards a stile over a wall. Cross this and follow the recently renovated path that climbs steeply up the left bank of Sour Milk Gill. Eventually the path swings left to go through a gate in a wall. Beyond this the angle eases. The craggy fell now rising prominently to your left is Base Brown. The renovated path ends around here but the well-trodden original path continues, gradually climbing and bearing left, around the foot of Base Brown, into the bare upland valley of Gillercombe. Across this valley towers imposing Raven Crag, known more commonly to climbers as Gillercombe Buttress.

The path eventually climbs leftwards out of Gillercombe to debouch onto the grassy saddle dividing Base Brown from Green

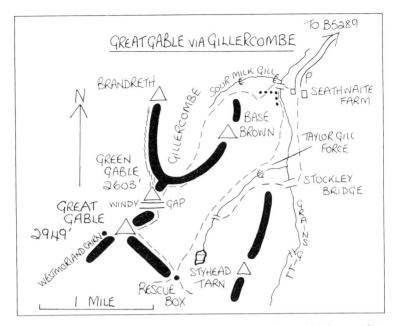

GREAT GABLE VIA GILLERCOMBE

Gable. Here it swings right and steepens, up increasingly rougher
ground, to emerge on a broad grassy ridge to the left of a prominent
rocky outcrop and near to an old fence post. The path from
Honister Pass, via Grey Knotts and Brandreth, joins from the far
side of the outcrop. Turn left now and follow the sanguine and
eroded path up easy grass to reach the summit of Green Gable.

A feature of the view from Green Gable is undoubtedly the
stark presence of Gable Crag across the narrow saddle of Windy
Gap. To its right, framed in the saddle of Beckhead, is distant
Scatallan with, given a clear day, the ethereal outline of the Isle of
Man floating beyond. The flattish fell to the right of Beckhead is
Kirkfell. Rightwards of Kirkfell bulky Pillar towers over the dark
regimented conifers of Ennerdale and the silvery bends of the
Liza. Thrusting out of its Ennerdale flank is the spiky summit of
famed Pillar Rock.

Bear left from the summit cairn and follow the steep shaly path
down into Windy Gap. Climb leftwards up the far slope along a
narrow path which leads to the foot of steeper ground. Slabby
rocks now lead up onto the bouldery dome of Gable where the
angle eases and soon the cairn on its plinth of boulders is reached.
As you approach take note of the memorial plate to the war dead
of the Fell and Rock Club attached to one of these boulders. Every
Remembrance Sunday walking and climbing folk gather here to
pay tribute.

The spread of Gable's dome restricts the view. Given a clear day continue your line of approach past the cairn and down a short way to find the Westmorland Cairn, which is perched on the dizzy rim of Westmorland Crag. From it there is a superb bird's-eye view of Wasdale Head's cramped fields pinned down by a network of walls. Beyond, the Screes plunge precipitously into the gleaming depths of Wastwater. I saw my first mountain sunrise from Gable top. I chiefly remember an older, learned, friend polishing his specs, peering myopically eastwards and saying, 'Remarkable. In texture and colour exactly like the underside of a male newt in the breeding season'.

To descend from Gable's cairn head south-easterly, or leftwards as you face the memorial tablet, following an eroded path down rough but relatively easy-angled ground to reach Styhead Pass near the Mountain Rescue Box. Turn left here and follow the broad path past the austere waters of Styhead Tarn. Continue with this path along the left bank of Styhead Gill until a footbridge over the gill is reached. You have a choice of route now. Either, continue down the left bank and eventually a scrambly path down the rocky left bank of Taylor Gill, giving a splendid view of Taylor Gill Force, then curving left around the lower slopes of Base Brown to join your outward route below Sour Milk Gill. Or, cross the footbridge and follow an eroded path down to and over Stockley Bridge before turning down-valley and easily back to Seathwaite Farm. The former is more interesting, the latter easier.

BUTTERMERE

The Buttermere Trio

A delightful ridge walk. Once the crest is gained the going is easy, with an old fence to aid navigation. The all round views are splendid, but the 'bird's-eye' views into Bleaberry and Burtness Combes and upon Buttermere and Crummock Water are superb.

Parking: The car park to the right (behind) of the Fish Hotel, Buttermere (GR 174169).

TURN right in front of the Fish Hotel then right again on the path behind the hotel's private car park. Follow this path across the fields, ignoring a right fork signposted 'Scale Bridge/Scale Force', towards the silvery thread of Sour Milk Gill spilling down the wooded flank of Red Pike. A footbridge takes you over Buttermere Dubs, the beck linking the lakes. Beyond it a 'Red Pike' sign points left to a smaller footbridge, followed by a kissing-gate between a wall and fence at the edge of the lake. Beyond this a path zig-zags up through the trees to a crossing path signposted 'Red Pike/Lakeshore'.

Now climb the recently rebuilt 'Red Pike' path slanting leftwards through the trees. It is a solidly constructed piece of work and a vast improvement on the former eroded trough. Above the tree line the path climbs left then right up the steep fellside. The angle eases as it passes through an old wall and a threadbare line of equally ancient trees to reach the bank of Sour Milk Gill. Paths on either side of the beck lead to the shore of Bleaberry Tarn. Bleaberry Combe is yet another of Lakeland's elegantly sculpted upland hollows whose beauty is enhanced by a tarn. It is marred only by the badly eroded path slashing like an open wound the breast of Red Pike, an unfortunate fate that all fine fells suffer. Scramble up this steep mountain highway to reach the cairn capping the summit of Red Pike. Five lakes, Ennerdale Water, Crummock Water, Loweswater, Buttermere and Derwentwater can be spotted by the vigilant. Arrayed in splendour across the head of Crummock Water are the lovely Grasmoor group. Some years ago, on an exceptionally clear day, Ben Lomond was spotted from Red Pike, a distance of 120 miles.

Now head on to High Stile. The rusting remains of an old boundary fence will be met just south of and below the summit of Red Pike. In mist this is a useful aid to navigation as it stays with

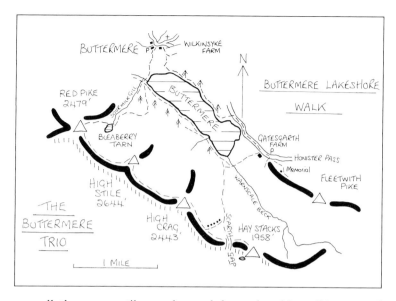

you all the way until you descend from the ridge. Given good weather keep as close as possible to the precipitous north-eastern rims of these fells for the 'bird's-eye' views of tarn and lakes, often framed between steep gully walls. A pleasant undulating walk of about a mile leads south-easterly around the rim of Bleaberry Combe and up to the bouldery summit of High Stile. En route the rock changes from the pinky granite, or granophyre, which gives Red Pike its name, to the greyer and more familiar Borrowdale volcanic.

High Stile is rugged, bouldery, and multi-cairned. According to the cartographer a cairn on the north-eastern spur, splitting Bleaberry from Birkness (Burtness) Combe, is one metre higher than the cairned eminence crowning the rim of Chapel Crags, above Bleaberry Combe. West-south-westerly, beyond the head of Ennerdale Water, the Isle of Man may be spotted above the summit of Lank Rigg. From the cairn perched on the very lip of Chapel Crags the 'bird's-eye' view is superb. Below, under the ugly path scar slashing Red Pike, lies dark Bleaberry Tarn. Beyond gleams Crummock Water, split from far Loweswater by the brawny hump of Mellbreak.

Descend alongside the old fence, south at first, then swinging south-easterly around the rim of Birkness Combe, to ultimately surmount the grassy summit of High Crag. Birkness Combe is not graced by a tarn but lined with magnificent crags which endow it with a special wild beauty. This is climber's country, from the dank overhangs of Eagle Crag to the sunnier slabs of Grey Crags. Every

111

fellwalker worth his or her salt should make an effort to visit this delectable corrie – one of Lakeland's finest.

By the time you've reached High Crag top, Gable's proud dome – and its pointy underling Green Gable – must be a familiar sight. Marching rightwards of them, above and beyond the bulky plateau of Kirkfell, are Ill Crag, Broad Crag, Scafell Pike and Scafell – three thousand footers all.

Descend south-easterly, still with the occasional fence post, down the steep and badly eroded scree and grass slope of Gamlin End. At the foot of Gamlin End turn left over the rim of the fell and follow a path down alongside walls to joint the Scarth Gap path where it passes through a wall gap. Turn left down this, and left at every fork below to join the lakeshore path. Beyond the footbridge over Comb Beck, below where it cascades out of Birkness Combe, the path forks. Take the right fork and every subsequent right fork along this delightful lakeshore path to reach your outward route at the kissing-gate by the water's edge.

The Buttermere Lakeshore Walk

Possibly the finest lakeshore walk in Lakeland. The path along the Hassness shore is particularly delightful.

Parking: As for Walk 36.

WALK back between the Bridge Hotel and farm buildings to the road. Turn right up the road to the entrance to Wilkinsyke Farm, signposted 'Lakeshore Path'. Turn into this, walk past the Sike Farm Shop, and on through the farmyard to a gate labelled 'Footpath'. Beyond this the path crosses fields above the lake. Across the valley Sour Milk Gill spills down the wooded flank of Red Pike. The summit of Red Pike cannot be seen, lying back beyond the rim of Bleaberry Combe. The crenellated crest of High Stile, however, thrusts into view, poised on the rim of Chapel Crags some two thousand three hundred feet above the waters of Buttermere. Red Pike, High Stile and High Crag present to the walker on the Hassness shore a mountain wall almost alpine in stature and structure. A gate is reached signposted 'Bridleway/ Lakeshore'. Follow the lakeshore path rightwards to negotiate a steep rocky section before swinging left onto the lakeshore. Look back to see the broad summit of Grasmoor rising above conical Whiteless Pike and the lowly but craggy ridge of Rannerdale Knotts.

Across the headwaters of the lake the upland combe of Warnscale Bottom is dominated by the dark tors and crags of Hay Stacks. Beyond a stile a notice informs that you are now on a 'permissive footpath' over private land. This path now wends along the wooded lakeshore, at one point passing through a narrow tunnel hacked through a rocky headland. Up through the trees on your left you will glimpse the cascades of Goat Gill and Hassneshow Beck spilling into impressive ravines. Eventually the path emerges from the trees to cross two flat fields, rounding the wall that divides them by a gate on the lakeshore. Across the lake now Comb Beck spills out of rugged Birkness Combe. In the upper reaches of the combe look for the steep rocks and pointed summit of Eagle Crag. Distance diminishes its size but Eagle Front, a classic 500 foot climb on this crag, was featured in the television series 'Lakeland Rock', being climbed by Chris Bonington and the late Bill Peascod, a pioneer of many superb climbs on the Buttermere crags. Further right, you can now glimpse the summit cone of Red Pike.

A gate leads out of the second field and along a path above the water to shortly emerge on to the road. Turn right, along the road, towards Gatescarth Farm. Ahead rises 'Fleetwith Edge', the steep north-west ridge of Fleetwith Pike. Low down on this ridge you may spot a white cross at the foot of a crag. It marks the spot where an unfortunate Victorian girl lost her life, apparently as a result of tripping over her 'fell-pole'. Fell poles were the Lakeland equivalent of an alpenstock and 'de rigueur' in Victorian fell walking circles, and even earlier. Coleridge felt himself inadequately equipped for a walking expedition without one and virtually wrestled with his wife for her broom handle before setting out. Turn right at Gatescarth Farm through the gate signposted 'Public Bridleway – Ennerdale/Buttermere' and also 'Rescue Post'. Walk between a fence and wall before turning left with the fence to a gate. Beyond this follow a path alongside a wall, then a fence, where there is a contribution box to the Cockermouth Mountain Rescue Team, and into the fields at the head of the lake.

Continue through a gate, over a bridge spanning the Warnscale Beck, then up to and through a gate signposted 'Public Bridleway – Ennerdale via Scarth Gap/Buttermere'. Turn right to follow the latter path to where it crosses a footbridge over Combe Beck, spilling out of Birkness Combe in a series of fine cascades. Beyond the bridge the path forks. Follow the right fork down along the lakeshore to a gate leading into the woods, signposted 'NT Burtness'. Follow a path through woods along the lakeshore to climb to a fork. Turn right and down again to the lakeshore. This path is particularly enjoyable on a clear late winter afternoon or a summer evening, with the Grasmoor fells, gilded with sun and brushed with shadow, rising across the gleaming water. When the path forks right near the end of the lake follow it down to the water's edge to pass through a kissing-gate between a fence and wall. Walk right, across two footbridges spanning becks, and follow the well-worn path right across the fields, to enter Buttermere village past the private car park of the Fish Hotel.

CRUMMOCK

Whiteless Pike and Grasmoor

Grasmoor is King of the Mountains in north-west Lakeland. Big, bluff, ruddy, like a Henry the Eighth surrounded by a bevy of shapely consorts. There are a variety of interesting ways up and down it. This is not the easiest, nor the hardest, but a good one. You'll enjoy it.

Parking: In the 'Cinderdale Car-Park' on the verge of the B5289, below Grasmoor. (GR 163194).

FOLLOW the 'Footpath' fingerpost at the rear of the car-park across the common to Cinderdale Beck. Cross the beck and follow the path towards a rounded tree-topped crag on the skyline. Pass below this crag and continue towards the narrow valley of Rannerdale, (see Walk 39), its mouth dominated by the craggy pyramid of Rannerdale Knotts. When the path forks, near a metal 'Path' sign, turn right across a footbridge spanning the Rannerdale Beck. Climb up to and over a stile in a wall and turn left alongside the wall.

Higher up the valley the path crosses on to the left bank of Squat Beck before surmounting the narrow grassy saddle at its head. A cairn marks the junction of several paths. Ahead, the great bulk of Robinson, rising between the cleft of Newlands Hause and the depths of Buttermere, blocks the view. Look back for a glimpse of Crummock Water, with Loweswater gleaming beyond. Turn left and climb the path zig-zagging steeply upwards. The angle eases when Whiteless Breast is surmounted, but steepens again for the final climb on to the narrow summit of Whiteless Pike.

The views are wide ranging in every direction but northwards, where Grasmoor fills the sky. North-easterly Wandope, Sail, Scar Crags and Causey Pike jut into the valleys of the Sail and Rigg becks. South-south-easterly the distant peaks are of Lakeland's finest. Left to right are Bowfell, Esk Pike, Great End, where the skyline is blocked by Gable's dome, before Scafell Pike and Scafell rear their loftier heads.

The drop into Saddle Gate is followed by the ascent of Whiteless Edge. This 'edge' is a slender ridge with a sense of great depth on either hand but it presents no difficulty that cannot be overcome simply by placing one foot in front of the other. It leads to a cairn

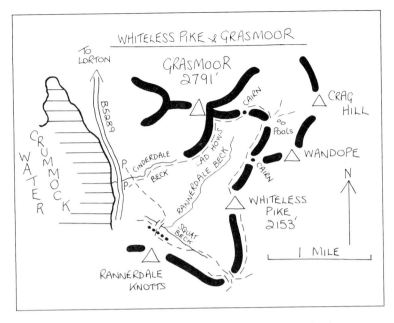

on a prominence on the south-west corner of the sloping grassy plateau of Wandope Moss, whose summit, Wandope, rises away to your right. Ahead, to your left, looming out of the depths of Rannerdale Beck, and nearly four hundred feet higher, is Grasmoor, your target for today. The fell rising ahead and to your right is Crag Hill.

The path descends slightly before cutting across the slope falling into Rannerdale Beck to reach a junction of paths near some small boggy pools in the grassy saddle between Grasmoor and Crag Hill. Now turn left, west-north-west, and climb a worn path to a large cairn. The path beyond cuts across the head of a shaly slope dropping with increasing steepness towards the Rannerdale Beck. The far side of this slope is bounded by a grassy spur dropping away to your left. This is the head of the Lad Hows ridge, your way down. Pass above the spur and to the right of two prominent cairns to shortly reach the sprawling cairn-cum-wind shelter crowning the summit of Grasmoor.

The view from the summit is so extensive that space does not permit a detailed description. Look down onto the lovely dark gleaming lakes set in a ring of fells that time and weather have carved and polished into a rare finish, and visualise the medieval 'secret fortress'. Curiously, from here, Gable's usually dominant dome merges into the rugged backcloth of the loftier Scafells. If the day is fine, walk north-easterly across the summit plateau to

116

reach the rim of Dove Crags. Across the gulf of Gasgale Gill the deeply eroded gullies of Whiteside, spewing ashen scree, would make a fitting backcloth to a 'spaghetti' western.

To descend, retrace your steps until you have passed to the left of the second sizeable cairn perched on the fell rim. Now turn right on to the grassy spur which steepens into a stony ridge. Despite the rough ground underfoot there is a reasonable twisty path. This steep stony ridge eventually eases out onto a broader heathery spur where the path becomes less obvious. Continue to where the butt-end of the spur is crowned by a small cairn. From it, bear down to the right on an improving path twisting down through the bracken to ultimately follow the tinkling cascades of Cinderdale Beck down to Cinderdale Common and your car.

Mellbreak

*When approached from Scalehill Bridge, Mellbreak appears as a
towering, weather-ravaged cone that belies its modest height. Get
closer and it soars even steeper. Lock grips with it and you'll find the
climb up its northern prow steep but full of interest. The summit is a
disappointment, but the climb and unfolding views are worth every
gasping breath.*

*Parking: In the National Trust free car park in Lanthwaite Wood,
near Scalehill Bridge, on the road between Lorton and Loweswater.
(GR 149215).*

WALK over Scalehill Bridge towards Loweswater, where the road
forks by a telephone box. Mellbreak towers ahead and Crummock
Water gleams beyond the hedges to your left, with Gable's far
dome crowning the dalehead. Turn left at the telephone box and
past the church to a junction. Turn down left then almost immediately right, 'No Through Road', to pass behind the Kirkstile Inn.
The tarmac ends at Kirkgate Farm and a rough walled lane leads
on. Look back across the valley to the towering cone of Grasmoor
End, slashed by the Y-shaped Lorton Gully. Where the lane veers
left a peek over the wall on your right reveals a lumpy field. These
are ancient earthworks which appear to have more purpose when
seen from the prow of Mellbreak. Remember to look! The lane
ends at a gate where paths fork. Climb left, between trees, then on
up the fellside to the foot of the rock, scree and heather looming
above. Pause by a cairn at the foot of a fan of pinky scree for a
'breather'. Look back on to Loweswater nestling in its woody
hollow. Beyond, the distant Scottish uplands rise above the waters
of the Solway Firth.

Climb the path which serpentines up through scree fans and
heather banks to the left of a deeply eroded and shaly groove.
A final slant left leads to and around a rocky pinnacle on the
skyline. Behind this a rock stairway leads to a cairn and a superb
'bird's-eye' view of the Vale of Lorton. A steep heathery climb left
leads onto the summit ridge. Here, step left and right around
a rocky corner for one of the finest 'surprise' views in Lakeland.
Below, Crummock Water, Buttermere, and their delectable cirque
of fells do their damnedest to emulate a Norwegian fiord. They
don't quite succeed, but it's an impressive effort. Worth every
accelerated heart-beat and lung-rasping breath.

Step back and climb easily up to Mellbreak's northern top, a
disappointingly broad and grassy dome.

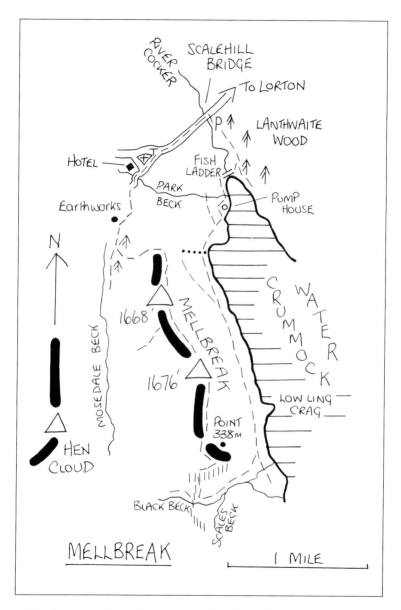

MELLBREAK

1 MILE

Northwards, there is a panoramic view of the Solway. South-easterly, over and beyond the fell's southern top, is High Stile, with Red Pike's cone to its right. Behind Red Pike peeks Pillar. To the left of High Stile looms Gable, the V-gash of Windy Gap, and

Green Gable. Below and left of Gable, Hay Stacks and Fleetwith Pike curve around the headwaters of Buttermere. Across Crummock Water, the medieval battleground of Rannerdale lies in the shadow of the rocky spur of Rannerdale Knotts. Walk a little way east of the cairns for the view down on to Crummock Water, dominated by the massive pinky-grey dome of Grasmoor.

Legend has it, and novels have been based upon this tale, that the medieval defenders of Buttermere lured an invading Norman army into the confines of Rannerdale, to ambush and slaughter. It was a radio adaptation of one of these novels, 'The Secret Fortress' by Joyce Reason, on Children's Hour (that dates me!), that first lured me, a history-mad teenager, to Lakeland.

To reach the slightly higher south top follow a path skirting the western edge of the boggy saddle dividing the tops. Ignore the path forking right, down into Mosedale, and follow the fainter path climbing left on to the south top. As you climb look right for a possible glimpse of the Isle of Man floating between Hen Comb and Great Borne.

Descend southwards, passing between tottery old fenceposts, to where the ridge steepens down into a hollow behind a hummock, marked 338 metres on the 2½″ map. Go to the right of the hummock, then left above a hollow, then over the rise beyond to a fence. Turn right and follow the fence to two stiles. Cross the first stile and follow a fence down to a path alongside Black Beck. Turn left and follow this path alongside the beck to eventually meet the lakeshore path where it crosses the beck.

Turn left and follow this path to shortly pass the promontory of Low Ling Crag – an idyllic spot for an impromptu picnic and swim. Across the lake towers massive Grasmoor, its Lads How ridge (Walk 38) curving down between the ravines of Cinderdale and Rannerdale Becks. Whiteless Pike peeks over the craggy crest of Rannerdale Knotts, both peaks enfolding the once bloody defile of Rannerdale.

Beyond the promontory the path passes below the precipitous Crummock flank of Mellbreak and subsequently through the drainage from the broad grasslands above. It can become a bit squelchy hereabouts. Your target is a stile at the foot of the wall climbing the fellside ahead. Cross this and continue around the shore, ultimately to walk around a lovely little bay giving a superb view up the glistening stretch of Crummock Water to Hay Stacks and Gable.

Beyond the bay, climb over a promontory with a lakeshore fringe of trees and down to a stile. Beyond this, walk alongside a concrete flood barrier. One December afternoon we were forced to slosh along the top of this barrier which was awash. Our crossing wasn't helped by a sly gusty wind. This barrier/path leads to a fenced-off Pump House. Walk left around the fence to a stile. Beyond this follow the wooded and concrete-lined lakeshore. Cross a footbridge spanning Park Beck, which channels overspill from Loweswater into Crummock Water, before continuing along the lakeshore to the Fish Ladder. Cross the Fish Ladder, two footbridges linked by an island, walk past a wooden seat and turn left up a path through the wood to a path fork. Turn left again through Lanthwaite Wood to your car.

On the same December afternoon, we found the Fish Ladder under roaring waist high water. We had to beat a retreat and re-cross the Park Beck. We then walked alongside the beck to re-cross it at a higher footbridge. The path beyond led us to Muncaster House where a farm road led to a junction with our outward route near Scalehill Bridge.

WASDALE

Scafell Pike and Lingmell

*The walk described below is the shortest and easiest route to England's
highest mountain. A return over Lingmell, however, will add a
touch of adventure to your walk. Try and choose a clear day for the
joy of this walk is not only in 'bagging' the Roof of England but
in thrilling to the superb views, awesome from Lingmell, spread
before you.*

*Parking: On the green, near the old schoolhouse, Wasdale Head.
(GR 187085).*

WALK back along the road to a stile on your left, signposted 'The
Scafells'. Follow the path across scrubby fields to a footbridge
spanning the Lingmell Beck. Cross the bridge and climb right,
around the foot of the Lingmell Spur, your eventual descent route,
to join the path from Brackenclose and the Campsite, on the bank
of Lingmell Gill. Your adrenalin will begin to flow as you round
the corner and see the fretted skyline crowning the head of the gill.
Climb alongside the gill, crossing it eventually where it splits at the
foot of a grassy spur called Brown Tongue. The climb up Brown
Tongue is tedious but as the angle eases the view ahead excites.

Brown Tongue widens and eases out into a spectacular, boulder-
strewn amphitheatre known as Hollow Stones. Ahead, slung between
awesome Scafell Crag and the more amiably inclined buttresses of
Pikes Crag, is the gap known as Mickledore, 'the Great Door'.

Follow the worn path which forks left, climbing below the stony
skirts of Pikes Crag towards the gap (the Lingmell Col), dividing
Scafell Pike from Lingmell. Before reaching the Lingmell Col,
however, your path climbs steeply right round the northern rim of
Pikes Crag and starts its stony serpentines on to the summit dome
of man-trap boulders.

When close to the massive cairn, your path joins the path ascending
from Mickledore, then the two paths continue to the summit as one.
Should the summit be shrouded in mist make careful note of this
junction for your return journey. Liberally piled as it is with 'look-
a-like' boulders and cairns the summit of Scafell Pike can be a
confusing place in poor conditions, especially for the inexperienced.

The view, on a clear day, is so extensive I have not the space to
describe it in detail. South-west, across the gap of Mickledore, rise

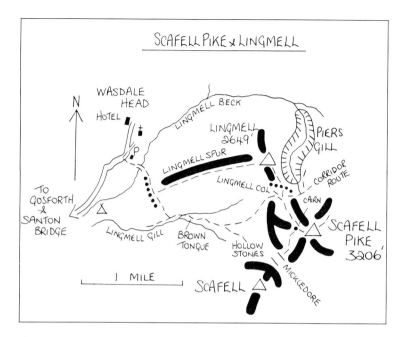

SCAFELL PIKE & LINGMELL

the rocky ramparts guarding the rounded summit of Scafell. Below and to the right of Scafell gleams Wastwater with, if you are very lucky, the Isle of Man balanced high above it on leagues of shining sea. Northwards, thrusts the shaly runnelled cone of Great Gable. To the left of Gable, peeking over the rim of Scafell Pike's dome, is Lingmell, your next objective.

Return by your way of ascent until just above the Lingmell Col. Look for a path forking right and down on to this saddle and follow it down. Walk through a gap in the wall bisecting the Col and climb the short but steepish grassy ridge on to the rock-strewn summit of Lingmell. This humble summit is invariably ignored by the massed pilgrims heading for Scafell Pike. It's their loss and your gain, for as well as being a 'tick' on your list of 'two-thousands' climbed it offers two enthralling and unusual views. Walk to the fell rim and peer down into the mighty shadowed cleft of Piers Gill. In the 1920's a gentleman, aptly named Crump, fell into Piers Gill and incredibly survived his injuries and managed to exist for eighteen days on a slab of fruit cake and a nearby trickle of water, before being found.

Walk along to the rocky knoll beyond the summit. Across the depths towers Gable, an heroic mountain, proudly bearing the scars of time and weather.

To descend, you can either return to the Lingmell Col and

reverse your route of ascent. Or, head westerly to pick up a path which veers south-westerly and down to pass through a gap in an old wall. It continues down a broad easy-angled ridge, with Wastwater beckoning ahead and below you. Eventually this ridge narrows and steepens, forming the Lingmell Spur which takes you down to a junction with your outward route on the bank of Lingmell Gill.

Middle Fell and Seatallan

This walk is the reverse side of Wasdale fellwalking. Gentler terrain, less worn paths, uncrowded summits, an unpretentious tarn, modest but pleasing waterfalls, and less dramatic but nonetheless rewarding views. In other words, a most enjoyable walk.

Parking: In the lay-by on the left just past the turn-off to Gosforth. (GR 151054).

WALK back down the road and turn right along the road to Gosforth, towards Greendale Farm. Your target is the path climbing above Greendale Farm alongside Greendale Gill. Before reaching the farm, however, you may spot a path short-cutting through the bracken on your right which links with the gillside path above the farm.

Continue up the path alongside the gill, which enfolds some lovely cascades, to where a path forks right. Turn right here on to a steepish climb, twisting through rocky outcrops, which ultimately leads you onto the summit of Middle Fell. As you climb you will see Greendale Tarn below and to your left. Now, if the mountain gods are blessing you with a fine clear day, find a sunny corner in which to take your well-earned rest. Feast your body upon 'butties' and your eyes upon mountains.

Having said this I have to admit that I cannot describe the view from Middle Fell, having never seen it! Every ascent I've made of this fell has been on a 'dreich' day, with the summit impaled deep into scudding, rain-swolled clouds. I do remember a momentary but awesome glimpse of The Screes through a wind-ripped hole in the murk.

There is a tale, probably apocryphal, that many decades ago a mass of rock, reputedly as big as St. Paul's Cathedral, broke away from the crags of The Screes and roared down into the lake. The noise and the 'tidal wave' frightened the folk of Wasdale into believing the day of reckoning had come and they hurriedly arranged for a special service to be held in the diminiutive church.

From the fell's position, the recommendations of friends, and the fleeting glimpses I've had through 'cloud windows', I'm aware this fell is worth the effort for its views over Wastwater, The Screes, and the magnificent cirque of high fells above Wasdale Head. So far, it's given me some needed exercise and a saving of money on film. I hope you are luckier.

MIDDLE FELL and SEATALLAN

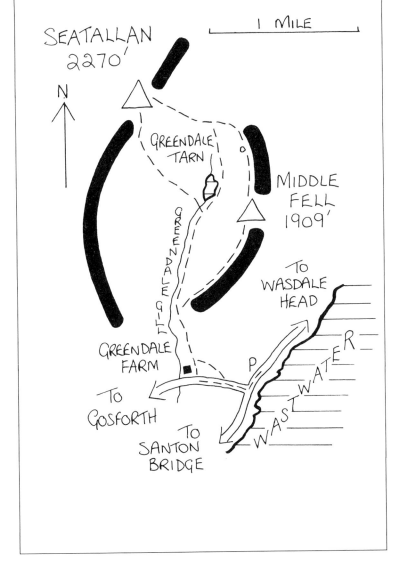

SEATALLAN
2270'

1 MILE

N

GREENDALE
TARN

MIDDLE
FELL
1909'

GREENDALE GILL

TO
WASDALE
HEAD

GREENDALE
FARM

P

WASTWATER

TO
GOSFORTH

TO
SANTON
BRIDGE

Descend along the obvious ridge. After passing a tiny tarn the path veers left and down through rocky outcrops to debouch on to the grassy saddle below Seatallan. (It's possible to 'escape' from the walk here, should you feel the need, by turning left down to Greendale Tarn and so down to Greendale Farm.

A faint path climbs steepish grass slopes before easing onto the broad grassy summit dome of Seatallan. The trig-point and wind shelter-cum-cairn stand on the far (westerly) rim.

For the reasons already given I'm unable to give a detailed description of the view. From both the summit of Glaramara and Green Gable, Seatallan pops up quite impressively, framed in the gaps of Styhead and Beckhead, with the Isle of Man moored on the horizon beyond it. So I assume the view from Seatallan, in reverse, of the more inland fells, and of Man, is equally rewarding.

Descend south-easterly down grassy slopes to where Greendale Gill spills out of Greendale Tarn. Boulder-hop across the gill on to the path that takes you back down to Greendale Farm.